THE HOLY MOUNTAIN

OF

LA SALETTE

THE MOST REVEREND WILLIAM ULLATHORNE

ARCHBISHOP OF BIRMINGHAM

Preserving Christian Publications Inc.
Albany, New York
2000

Imprimi potest: PAUL M. REGAN, M.S.
Praepositus Provinciae
Septem Dolorum Americae Septentrionalis

Nihil Obstat: JOHN J. COLLINS
Censor Librorum

Imprimatur: EDMUND F. GIBBONS,
Episcopus Albaniensis

Published by: **Preserving Christian Publications, Inc.**
Post Box 6129,
Albany, New York 12206

First Printing	June, 1996
Second Printing	October, 1996
Third Printing	May, 1997
Fourth Printing	May, 2000
Printed in India at:	Anaswara Printing & Publishing Co., Cochin - 682 018, India

ARCHBISHOP WILLIAM BERNARD ULLATHORNE

PREFACE

"Most Holy Father, on the 19th of September, 1846, a Lady appeared to me; they say it is the Blessed Virgin; you will judge whether it was by what follows."

— Maximin Giraud

The publishers of *The Holy Mountain of La Salette* have undoubtedly exercised their fair share of patience in awaiting this brief preface to the reprinting of Bishop Ullathorne's excellent treatise, which originally appeared in 1854. The slow influx of supplementary material, the deliberation over how to deal with the secret of Melanie and a full measure of procrastination all blended to yield this manuscript well beyond the due date. For this delay I beg their indulgence.

September 19, 1996 marks the sesquicentennial of the apparition of the Lady in Tears to two young shepherd children, Melanie Mathieu (Calvat), aged fourteen, and Maximin Giraud, aged eleven, in a remote hamlet nestled within the French Alps. The message she conveyed to them, as well as the mission she enjoined upon them with her parting words, "Well, my children, you will pass this on to all my people," have not failed to reach our own ears 150 years later. It is to the credit of Preserving Christian Publications, Inc. that her people have, in the re-issue of *The Holy Mountain of La Salette,* yet another source from which to draw a renewed knowledge of, and piety towards, their Queen and their Mother.

But perhaps I have already trodden too far. For Bishop Ullathorne, in deciding to investigate the events of that September day in 1846, undertook the endeavor with no preconceived notions. To be sure, his interest was great; but so too was his objectivity. His book unfolds a story from investigation to personal conviction, and everything in-between. A contemporary of the apparition, he was able to garner his information from its very sources, down to the two children themselves. And when evidence has been previously gathered by others in the form of recorded dialogues, testimonies and evaluations, the good bishop contents himself with merely presenting the facts to the readers, with perhaps a short but noteworthy explicative. Such is the case, for example, in his eight-page reproduction of an extract from Bishop Dupanloup's letter, an incisive analysis of the character and replies of the two young seers under the intensive scrutiny of several years.

At the time of the original publication of *The Holy Mountain of La Salette,* the universal Church had not, in fact, yet rendered her verdict on the authenticity of the Blessed Virgin's appearance at that site. Hence the reader, even if he or she be non-Catholic or skeptical of the apparition, is given an intriguing insight into the procedures, both canonical and clinical, surrounding the ecclesiastical investigations of what are known as private revelations. And the search for truth is not without its lighter moments, as can be seen in the brief exchange found in the chapter entitled "Examination of the Children":

A curé interrupted (Melanie's) narrative of the event: "The Lady disappeared in a cloud?"

Melanie: "There was no cloud." The curé insists: "But it is easy to surround oneself with a cloud, and disappear."

Melanie: "Then do you, Sir, surround yourself with a cloud, and disappear."

Which brings us to another aspect of the apparition, what modern man would call the intangibles, where measurement is made of the world of the spiritual rather than the corporeal, where quantity fails and quality sustains. For there is a charm to the personalities and events at La Salette which the persevering reader will doubtless discover in this book. The disarming simplicity of the children imbues the entire story. Says Maximin to Melanie on discerning the Lady seated, face in hands, within the globe of light: "Keep your stick: I will take care of mine: if it does anything to us, I will give it a good knock!" The beautiful Lady's garb is both of this world and of another: a peasant-like robe, apron and headdress, yet all suffused with an indescribable light. She speaks at first in French, then switches to the local dialect, or patois, on observing the children's bewilderment at the French word for 'potatoes': "Ah, my children, you do not understand: I will say it in a different way." Tears flow continuously from her eyes as she sits, then stands so close to the two as to be within grasp.

But with simplicity, the quintessential attribute of God, comes the Cross. The children's accounts are misrepresented and twisted. The renowned Curé of Ars, St. John Vianney, becomes disillusioned after his encounter with Maximin, thereby shaking the faith of many in the apparition. The secrets entrusted to each of the seers constitute a burden and a source of incessant inquiry. But to tell more would be to tell the entire saga; let the truly impartial reader weigh the motives of credibility, as Bishop Ullathorne guides him through each episode.

In fine, it is the Cross of Christ which overshadows and lusters with truth the events of La Salette. Our Lady is seen to wear it upon her breast, flanked by the hammer of the Crucifixion of her Son and the pliers of His Descent from the Cross — without question her two greatest sorrows. She emerges from a globe of light at the very hour of First Vespers of the Feast of her Seven Dolors, as Léon Bloy observes. (I could not help but reflect, on learning of this remarkable concurrence, that the canonical hour of First Vespers — recited on the eve of a feast — was among the first jewels of the Catholic liturgy to be lost in the reforms of 1961.) She sheds torrents of sparkling tears in an effort to bring man to penance and to the observance of his most basic duties to God — respect for His holy Name and His holy Day. Her menace of bad wheat and rotten grapes portends — with no real stretch of the imagination — what the enemies of the Cross would soon accomplish regarding her Divine Son's clean oblation of the altar. And the two words of which Melanie inquired in committing her secret to writing — "Antichrist" and "infallibly" — provide clues sufficient to see in times to come the ever-darkening shadow of the Cross upon the children of the Sorrowful Mother.

She sat, so claimed the children, on the "Paradise" — the toy heaven made by them of stone and flowers. And so she does for each of us. The royal Way of the Cross is her message, and Paradise is the Cross.

May we love her to death, and throughout eternity.

— Father Joseph F. Collins
Feast of Corpus Christi
1996

Contents

Illustrations

INTRODUCTION

In the month of May, 1854, the writer of this book left England in company with three friends to visit the Holy Mountain of La Salette. Though impressed already with all I had read or heard of an event, which had proved the source of conversion or of consolation to so many thousands of Catholics, I resolved to take no further impressions from books written on the subject, as an immediate preparation. By the Divine Mercy, I received consolations on that Mountain which deepened the interest I had already taken in its mystery. I had the best opportunity of conversing with most of those persons who, from the beginning, have been concerned with the subject, its history, and its investigation; and especially with those whose names are most before the public, or who have had the care and direction of the Children. I had interviews with the Children of the Apparition themselves.

During my enquiries, I more than once suspended my judgment, and cautiously revised the grounds of my conclusions. I spoke with able men who held various degrees of doubt, as well as with earnest believers. And for this purpose I had peculiar facilities afforded me. And ever since I left the Holy Mountain, I have felt a strong desire urging me to impart to the Catholics of England more detailed information than they possess of this remarkable event of our times — remarkable, if we do no more than consider the great spiritual results which have flowed from it. Mr. Northcote's pamphlet has done something, but it is little more than an introduction to a subject, at that time scarcely known in England beyond a few vague reports. My duties will not allow me time to draw out as full a statement, or to argue it as completely, as I could wish to do. But I will do something towards it. And for more ample information, I must refer my readers to the able works already published in France.

William Bernard Ullathorne,
Archbishop of Birmingham

CHAPTER I

FROM LYONS TO CORPS

Departing from Lyons, city of early martyrs, and center of the great missionary work of modern days, our pilgrimage more properly begins. Not, indeed, with the discomforts of the ancient footsore pilgrim, but that there we left behind us for a time railroads, correspondence, newspapers, and other mundane distractions of the kind, and felt grateful for that comparative isolation which yielded a precious quiet for disposing and preparing the mind.

Here the pilgrim must turn aside to the Grande Chartreuse, if but to withdraw himself further from the world, and to deepen the devotion of his heart. Nor is this alien from the pilgrim's one object; for the children of the Apparition have made retreats under the direction of the fathers of the great monastery; and valuable information on La Salette may be gathered in these lofty solitudes. As we take the first ascent, everyone we meet points his fingers to one high peak on the right, covered from its base, as well as crowned, with forest. And on everyone's tongue is the name of the eloquent Lacordaire. On that high point is a tall cross, scarcely visible, it looks so thin in the blue and bright sky. It marks the spot behind which that reviver of the French Dominicans has placed his brethren, who in that lovely retirement, are preparing themselves for their spiritual combats with the world.

The road for ten miles runs through a valley flanked with wooded mountains, and presenting many points of remarkable beauty. At St. Laurent du Pont mules are in requisition, and at a mile beyond, the huge mountains begin to close upon the stream of the Guiers Mort, and the ascent begins in earnest. We reach the point of the old timber-built iron-forge, well known to artists, the single-span bridge, and the aged gateway. The steep and whitened precipices go up into the clouds, whilst their bases and ravines are full of the richest and most diversified foliage. The winding torrent, by which we ascend, rushes down its rocky bed, broken still more by great boulders agitated and covered with foam. The silver pines rise like dark giants, and go feathering up in places to the very summits. And the wonder is, how this countless number of vast stems, many with a hundred feet and more in their height, and with three or four feet in diameter above their roots, can find means to exist on the face of these huge precipices of naked rock, which seem as perpendicular as the trees that grow out of them.

Mile after mile the scene continues to rise more majestically upon the soul. I thought of the time when St. Hugo conducted his friend St. Bruno up these wild heights, when paths there were none, into his solitary retreat, where for six long years he dwelt with God alone in the midst of this marvellous creation.

The mountains at length receded on both sides, though reaching up to still greater altitude, whilst our way lay through dense forests of pines and beeches, mingling together the lightest with the darkest green, until at length, in the midst of an island of bright green meadow, the vast monastery of the Grande Chartreuse appeared. How tranquil it was! Beyond it rose the loftiest of these peaks, Le Grand Som, snow-capped, white as if blanched with age; and all around, in a vast circumference, beyond the forests of pine, rose other mountain peaks: "God's mountains, the eternal mountains!" I thought, as the sacred writer's words came upon my mind. The Grande Chartreuse is nature's Cathedral. The loftiest work of man is a toy by its side, and a speck from its summit. Here, for eight centuries, with one sad interruption, all that is sublime in contemplation has mingled with whatever is most terribly grand in God's creation.

In those cloisters the pilgrim passed six hours, which seemed to him but as one; for he had by his side that mild and meditative old man, upon whom has descended through so long and holy a line, the authority of St. Bruno. We spoke of that sainted founder, of his rule and of his disciples, and then of La Salette and its mystery. The General knew its history well, and the children thoroughly, and confided his remarks to the pilgrim. We walked together through those long and vacant cloisters. Two of them extended seven hundred feet in visible perspective, and the human form at the opposite extremity seemed almost lost from sight. No one was visible except the guest master, and now and then a single lay-brother, going on his errand recollectedly, with a beard like a prophet. There were forty monks still in the monastery, and eleven novices. But they were in their solitary cells, or in the equally solitary gardens allotted to each cell. Except in the choir at the divine offices, these contemplatives meet together but on special days for a time. From the hour of the midnight office, and after the short repose allowed between, their whole morning until mid-day is spent in pious exercises. There is no refectory. Each one's meal of meager diet is passed by a lay-brother from the cloister, through a little turn into his cell. We entered one which was unoccupied. Its two rooms were of fair size, were paved with old brick, and the plain walls were whitewashed.

The magnificent library was plundered by the revolutionists. It now forms the public library of Grenoble, one of the finest provincial libraries in France. The present collection at the monastery requires but a moderate-sized room. It is well supplied with the Fathers, and with the writers of the Order. The chapter-room is a fine apartment, parquetted and panelled with walnut, and adorned with copies of Le Sueur's celebrated series of pictures from the life of St. Bruno. The choir is remarkable only for its solemn severity of style and ornament. Its vault is circular; a high panelling of walnut along the walls, with a screen of the same height and material, encloses the stalls of the monks; and outside the screen are the stalls of the lay-brothers. There is no provision for the laity, but a door conducts to another chapel. Its altar was gaily ornamented for the Month of May. "This," said the General, "is for the family." "And who are the family?" "The servants of the monastery," he replied. It reminded one of the old Catholic kindliness and affection for domestics. In another portion of the cloister there is a beautiful little chapel built of marble and embellished with statues, at the cost of Louis XIII, and near it, in somewhat startling contrast is the funeral chapel for the obsequies of the brethren. The *reliques* chamber still contains the Holy Thorn deposited by St. Louis, as well as a portion of the True Cross brought from the East by the same holy king. This last is inserted in a metal ornament, Byzantine in character, on the two sides of which figures of St. Louis and Queen Blanche are raised. There are also some ancient relics, which, with these mentioned, the fathers contrived to conceal during the devastation of the monastery during the revolution.

Here, after a hospitable repast of monastic fare, remarkable for its exquisite cleanliness, we made the ascent to the solitude of St. Bruno. Half an hour brought us up through a path, a mile and a half in length, to a huge rock situated on the verge of a deep forest. Upon this, as its pedestal, stands a simple but picturesque chapel in the old circular style. Its interior is plain but adorned with frescoes. This chapel marks St. Bruno's retreat, and its position gives it a sublimity which elsewhere would not be felt. Near it is a vaulted fountain, into which the water falls with a strong gush from the opposite sides of the rock; this was St. Bruno's beverage. The spring supplies the monastery. The General could still speak of nineteen houses of the Order as under his jurisdiction. And at this very monastery six hundred priests had made their spiritual exercises in the course of the past year. But we must proceed on our pilgrimage.

Returning to Voreppe, our way continues through the most picturesque portion of the vale of Grésivaudan, by the side of the rapid Isére. It is bounded by mountains both precipitous and lofty, until Grenoble rises in view. We will not describe the magnificent situation of the old capital of Dauphiné, lodged in an amphitheater of mountains, between the Isére and the Drac. We will not stop to contemplate that singular citadel, piled fortress upon fortress for nine hundred feet, up the steep side of the mountain, round which we turn to enter the gates of the city. Let us hasten to the cathedral, that cathedral in which St. Hugo ministered and St. Francis of Sales preached. It was built by Bishop Isnardus at the close of the 10th century, after he had driven out the Saracens, as St. Hugo tells us in his chartulary, and is a solid and massive structure. Stripped, plundered, and made a witness of the most horrible scenes by the Huguenots, under the Baron of Adrets, but one object of interest beyond the bare walls has escaped their fury. On the epistle side of the chancel rises up the wall to the springing of the vault, rich with tracery and pinnacles, the tabernacle of the Blessed Sacrament, according to the medieval usage. The doors were of enamel, but only in part remain. Its use has ceased with the change of rite; and on that high altar where "the White Lamb celestial" reposes, the pilgrim offered the great sacrifice for his soul's good, and prayed for his brethren.

At Vizille, the memory of the desolating Huguenot again saddened, whilst it humbled the soul of the pilgrim. By a wonderful mercy that terrible Lesdiguiéres, whose castle looks so grim, died Catholic in his old age. Beyond Vizille we ascend steeply and slow-paced for two hours and a half, by the side of the expansive valley through which flows the Romanche. This valley is very beautiful, it had but recently thrown off its blanket of snow, and vegetation was pushing out vigorously. Snow still lay on portions of high mountains along its side. Beyond Laffrey, three mountain lakes, with their crisp waters of deep blue, are passed in succession. Here it was that Napoleon won over the first battalion sent out to stop his career from Elba. Beyond La Mure, the Alps send forth their giant arms to receive the traveller. Arthur Young has observed, that no portions of the Alps present scenes of more striking beauty than the southern parts of Dauphiné. Here the scenery begins to grow sublime in the highest degree, and the interest increases for the rest of the way. The roads, however hilly, are excellent. And now this road goes down, winding and turning upon itself like a huge serpent in broad meanders for several miles, until it narrows into a very deep-seated oval of rich vegetation, and then it goes up on the other side to greater heights with similar contortions. Look back. It is a prodigious hall sunk in the earth with giant staircases, and their balusters are beautiful trees. Vast and somber ranges rise upon the eye of the approaching traveller, crossing the line of the horizon in all directions, here fantastic in their form, there broken with sheer precipices thousands of feet in perpendicular.

At last Mount Obiou reveals himself distinctly above all his brethren. The masses of rock narrow stage above stage in their ascent, as the tower of Babel is represented, and the huge pile leans on one side, like the tower of Pisa, until the snow-covered summit has attained a height above the sea of nine thousand two hundred and twenty-five feet. It is said to be visible on the Mediterranean at a distance of one hundred leagues. Our way is not without its records of La Salette. There are vineyards as black, and, apparently, as lifeless as the withered fig-tree. And we pass through long lines of large walnut trees, their flowers all hanging dead and blackened on the branches which have not as yet shown a single leaf. These trees appear to be thus affected through one particular range of elevation in this part of the country.

At last the town of Corps appears. With its fifteen hundred inhabitants, it is situated on a platform in a nook of the mountains by the side of a cultivated space in which several valleys terminate. Behind it rises a singular-looking range, of which Mount Obiou is the principal feature. The approach is by a broad zig-zag before we can descend and cross the stream. The night is coming on; a storm of thunder shakes the mountains, the rain falls in torrents mingled with lightning; a long steep gully we are passing is alive with sheep, coming down in a skeltering run after their shepherds in quest of shelter. At last, though we heard that lives were lost in the storm, we are safe in Corps, on the eve of our Lord's Ascension.

THE BLESSED VIRGIN AS SHE FIRST APPEARED

CHAPTER II

THE ASCENT TO LA SALETTE

It is the Festival of our Lord's Ascension and I offered the Holy Sacrifice in the parish church of Corps. The people sang the *cantiques* with a simple and fervid piety. A Community of Sisters led the song, and amongst them was Melanie, professed under the name of Sister Mary of the Cross. A considerable number of persons communicated. At the convent of the Sisters of Providence I had an interview with the Superioress. Under her care the two children were placed at school, some months after the Apparition, and in that school they remained for four years. After some conversation Sister Mary of the Cross was introduced. She is now in her twenty-third year. Her features were pale but regular, her demeanor singularly modest and recollected, and her manner simple and religious. Her dark eyes are remarkably lustrous, and as she entered they brightened for an instant, though the rest of her features remained severely tranquil, and even in speaking she moved no more than her lips. Her whole expression gave me the idea of one who had suffered interiorly, and already tasted of the Cross. I put a series of questions to her, which she answered with calmness, but with readiness. And to this conversation we shall afterwards return.

The ascent to the Holy Mountain is about seven miles. At length our mules and guides are ready. An arm chair fixed on shafts, to be borne on men's shoulders, is prepared for an invalid of our party. The Abbé Mélin, Curé of Corps, and archpriest of the Canton, had the kindness to accompany us. This worthy ecclesiastic is a man of solid mind, and of the greatest prudence: few men are more respected. It was providential that such a man was found near, and with a certain authority, to watch over the whole affair of La Salette from the beginning, to moderate the circumstances which arose out of it, and to exercise a paternal care over the children. His conversation was highly interesting. And as he has observed in a published letter, he has "always been most strictly guarded in the information he has given on the Apparition, whether by speaking or writing, yet without giving up the truth, or failing in the courage of his conviction"; hence he observed, that though he has answered eight thousand letters on the subject, he has never experienced any unpleasantness from his correspondence.

Turning up the valley opposite that by which we entered Corps, with the towering Obiou behind us, we traced the path between the mountains and the stream for the distance of about a mile, and then crossing a bridge opposite the beautiful little chapel of Our Lady of Gournier, we ascend by a rocky mule path, carried close along the edge of the precipices. Below, on the right hand, at a depth of some hundred feet, was the rough bed of the stream, into which a number of cataracts were pouring their contributions. The air was full of this water-music. Thickly on each side grew oaks, firs, and pines. And above the trees, the mountains on each side exhibited that calcareous formation which is common to these regions, though the boulders in the streams are sometimes of granite. After winding for some two miles or more through this kind of scenery, we emerged upon a cultivated basin of considerable extent. Ten small hamlets lie dotted at irregular intervals over its surface, or seated in the corners of the mountain bases, each with its fringe of beech and ash. In the center stands the parish church, and each separate group of houses has its little chapel. This green basin is closed in on all sides by mountains, sloping upwards to a very great elevation. The cultivation goes up a fourth of their height, bordered by a broad belt of dark pines, after which all is bare and barren, with patches of snow. Skirting this crater-like formation, on its left, midway, we pass through the Ablandins, the hamlet in which the children were in employment at the time of the Apparition.

We reach the last of these hamlets; it is Dorsiéres, seated at the foot of the mountain named le Planeau, on the top of which a cross is to be seen. Here we parted with the last trees, a few sickly looking beeches and some small ashes, old, and curiously gnarled, and as yet without a leaf. We now begin to wind up round the right side of le Planeau, the high range of le Chamoux bending out on the other side of the ascent. It is a region of blue schist, with very little herbiage, and the whole steep ascent is broken all over with ravines. Into this silent region, beyond the dwellings of men, beyond the trees, beyond the birds, we ascend until we have rounded le Planeau, and have gained six thousand feet above the sea. One abrupt ascent more, by a straight path, and we reach the terrace *sous les Baisses*. Le Gargas still rises before us to a height of one thousand two hundred and fifty feet, on the south is le Planeau, still rising considerably, whilst, on the north-east, is le Chamoux, ascending higher than le Gargas. Here is a wonderful change; from the terrace to the top of the mountains all is covered with beautiful verdure, and enamelled with blue flowers. This terrace is the scene of the Apparition.

The bells of the sanctuary were ringing; the Missionary Fathers, backed by groups of pilgrims, stood on the verge with their cordial welcomes ... I hastened to the fountain; to that fountain which had gushed forth from the spot where stood our sorrowing Mother, with her crucified Son upon her breast. I now understand what is felt at Bethlehem, or at Nazareth, or on Calvary. But, here, time was effaced. The event was as of yesterday. Its spirit still breathed freshly on the spot. Here, in this solitude, withdrawn from the world of men, came a vision from Heaven, and a word spoken with tears of pity, has reverberated through the nations, and has shown its power by multiplied fruits. And its apostles were two poor and unknown children. (See Appendix - Note A.)

CHAPTER III

DEVOTIONS ON LA SALETTE

Four happy days we passed on this Mountain: this Mountain sanctified by Mary; sanctified by the perpetual Sacrifice of the Altar; sanctified by the Indulgences from the Sovereign Pontiff; sanctified by the piety and preaching of its Missionaries; sanctified by innumerable pilgrimages; and sanctified by countless prayers and repentances. The sanctuary of the church is alone completed. It is in form a basilica, in style romanesque. On one side of it rises the residence of the Missionary Fathers, on the other, that for the Sisters of the Apparition, who have care of the female pilgrims. These edifices are in character with the church, and are all built of black marble, obtained from the side of Mount Gargas. Every other material is brought up the whole ascent from Corps, on the backs of mules. The cost of erection is very great, and funds are yet wanted for commencing the nave, while the hospice, with its cloisters for the reception of pilgrims, is still but a plan on paper. Meanwhile, the Fathers do their best to accommodate those persons who come from great distances, and a temporary structure of wood has been erected for the reception of ladies. To their accommodation the Religious Sisters look with a kind and affectionate solicitude. They are most literally in *bivouac,* and you see ladies of various countries, and of all ranks, packed together; but the charity which reigns on this Holy Mountain compensates for everything.

The season had scarcely commenced when we arrived and snow had covered the mountain from a passing storm the day before. But in the second week of June there were seventy-five gentlemen at the table of the Fathers, and a still greater number of ladies with the Sisters. From June to the end of September, the average of arrivals is sixty persons a day, whilst on Sundays this number is augmented by a thousand or twelve hundred pilgrims from the neighboring parts of

the country. The kindness and attention shown by the Fathers at all
times, and to all classes of persons, is one of the beautiful features of
this Sanctuary. This spirit extends even to the least of the domestics
of the mission. And lest this should be supposed to be mercenary, I
ought to add, that these domestics when it was pressed upon them,
even in private, resolutely refused to receive any gratuity. "It is a
forbidden thing," they said. Though pilgrims were arriving at all
hours, yet their wants were immediately attended to, and no confusion
was manifest. "Ask for what we can give, and what we can do for you
at all times," was said to one of my fellow-travelers, "you know, when
you come to see your Mother, you are at home."

    We arrived a little before Vespers; and after the psalms were
sung in the temporary chapel, the procession filed out, first the
women, then the men, then the clergy. They sang the *Magnificat* and
the *Salve Regina*, forming two choirs beside the fountain. Then urged
by the Fathers, the pilgrim stood by the well, and in a language to
which he was unused, and which came uncouthly from his mouth, he
gave utterance to his emotions, and his fellow-pilgrims wept around
him. Then they returned for the benediction of the Most Holy, singing
canticles. The confessionals were much engaged. And the Fathers
commenced giving a retreat, in which they preached the great moral
truths with force and eloquence. On the Sunday, six hundred pilgrims
came up the Mountain at early morning. Of these three hundred and
fifty communicated. After a considerable number of masses in the
little temporary chapel, the last was said in the open air, on the scene
of our Lady's Ascension. Blocks of marble lay all about and served
for seats. Canticles were sung.... The Mountain is always resounding
with canticles, except in the long winter .... and then the long list of
notices for prayers was given out. These notices are given daily to the
pilgrims, morning and evening; and the invitations to pray for the
conversion of England comes even before the one for France. France
is everywhere devoted to prayer for England, especially in the South.
The nuns make a weekly communion for us; and in many parish

pulpits the recommendation is made every week. It was curious, and wakened more than one serious reflection in me, when Père Sibillat gave out that recommendation for England, to hear the echo from the mountains distinctly reply: "Pray for the conversion of England." The sermon followed.

In the interval between mass and vespers, groups of pilgrims were singing canticles; others the Litany of our Lady. Some were praying at the fountain, or drinking of its waters. Others were performing the Way of the Cross along the path which our Lady trod. All seemed most contented, and full of cheerfulness.

At vespers the long procession filed on to the favorite fountain. On one side of the ravine into which it flows, the women sat on the hill apart, round the banner of the Blessed Virgin, and behind the banner stood the Nuns; on the other side the men were arranged. There was a wide interval between. The Clergy occupied the two sides of the altar, placed on the verge of the ravine, and by the side of the Ascension. As verse followed verse of the psalms, hill responded to hill, the women to the men. Then on a Canon of the diocese of Meaux, standing by the fountain, preached an eloquent sermon, and the benediction was given in the chapel. After which the pilgrims of a day, snatched from their weekly toils, began to descend. "Oh," said a venerable English Catholic layman, who stood by me, "that England knew such things as these! Protestantism," he added, "is a cruel unbelief!"

I have spoken of the great beauty of the scene around the sanctuary. All the lines of the mountains which descend upon it, even where steepest, are soft and flowing, and covered with greensward. There is neither bush nor tree, but the surface is endlessly varied. Flowers are abundant, chiefly blue in color. There is the spring gentian and the stemless gentian, the mountain violet and the Alpine forget-me-not, and the mountain polygala; and, mixed with these, is the rock-cystus, the Alpine soldanella, and a small cowslip. Several kinds of ferns show themselves, and higher up the dwarf juniper is occasionally met with.

But it is from the top of le Gargas, where one looks down a depth of 1,300 feet upon the sanctuary, that the beauty of this chosen spot is best appreciated. All round is a vast and almost unlimited prospect of wild and barren ranges, whilst at that high elevation the scene of the Apparition, closed in with its own mountains, like an amphitheater, exhibits from the terrace of the fountain to the summits of the enclosing mountains, one vast carpet of green, variegated with its flowers, and is alone adorned with a verdure so rich, and with an aspect so soft. On the opposite side of le Gargas and le Chamoux, the precipices are sheer walls of naked rock, descending for a depth of some two thousand feet. And beyond lie chains of mountains, confused and heaped in all directions, on to the verge of the horizon, as dark as bronze or iron, and without a leaf, or a blade of grass apparent on their surface. Two or three narrow valleys, sunk to immense depths, are the only relief of this terrible wildness. "There," said the brigadier of the cantonal *gendarmerie*, who had ascended the mountain with us, pointing on the side of the sanctuary, "is a picture of Paradise; and there," he added, pointing on the other side, "is a picture of Hell." The broad and broken chasm which, on the opposite side, leads down to Corps, offers a contrast of another kind. "What a fine taste our Lady has!" . . . "How well our Lady has chosen." Such are the exclamations one often hears, as the pilgrims give utterance to the admiration which the place inspires. The sanctuary itself has not been erected on the immediate scene of the Apparition. The ground was unavailable, and for better reasons, it has been judiciously left in its natural state.

We will now proceed to the history of the Apparition. (See Appendix - Note B.)

THE SITE OF THE APPARITION

CHAPTER IV

THE TWO CHILDREN
BEFORE THE APPARITION

Peter Maximin Giraud was born at Corps, on the 27th of August, 1835, of poor parents. His father was a wheelwright. In September, 1846, his father sent him for a week, as an act of kindness, to guard the cows of his friend Peter Selme, a small farmer at the Ablandins, one of the hamlets of La Salette, the boy in his service being sick at the time. At that period Maximin was eleven years old. He was small for his age, but healthy and active. He was utterly without education, could neither write nor read, and when brought to the church for instruction would escape to play with his comrades; so that, as he had not received any religious instruction, he could not be admitted into the class preparing to make their first communion. His father declared that it had taken three or four years to teach him, and that with difficulty, to say the *Our Father* and the *Hail Mary*. Peter Selme describes him before the commission of enquiry, as he knew of him during the short time he was in his employment, to be "an innocent without malice, without foresight. Before he started with the cows to the mountain, we gave him his breakfast, and supplied his blouse or his sack with provisions for the day. And, to be sure, it has happened that we have come upon him on the way, and found he had already eaten his provisions and given a large share of them to the dog: and when we said to him, 'But what will you eat the rest of the day?' Maximin has answered, 'But I am not hungry'." When asked, some time after the event of his life, "Maximin, I am told, that before the Apparition of La Salette, you were somewhat of a story teller?" He smiled, and honestly said, "They have told you true. I told lies, and I swore when I flung stones after my strayed cows." Such was Maximin Giraud.

Frances Melanie Mathieu was also born at Corps, on the 7th of November, 1831. Her parents were of the very poorest, and at an early age she had to earn her bread by guarding cattle. She rarely entered a church, for her employers kept her at work on Sundays and festivals, as well as on week days. She had scarcely any knowledge of religion, and her ungrateful memory could not retain two lines of her catechism. For the nine months before the Apparition she had been in the employment of Baptiste Pra, another small farmer of the Ablandins. When this worthy man was interrogated as to her character, he described her "as excessively timid, and so careless of herself, that on returning from the mountain, drenched with rain, she never thought of changing her clothes. Sometimes, and it was a part of her character, she would sleep in the cattlesheds; and at others, if not observed, she would have passed the night under the stars." Baptiste Pra also observed, that, before the Apparition, Melanie was idle, disobedient, and inclined to pout, even so far at times as not to answer what was said to her. But after the Apparition she became active and obedient; and that she said her prayers better.

I must now extract from the formal depositions, which the two employers of the children made in the year 1847. They are drawn up by Dr. Dumanoir, doctor in law, and judge *suppléant* in the court of Montélimar. This gentleman had repeatedly visited La Salette, and had taken the most exact and minute informations on all that concerned the Apparition. The uprightness and character for truth of the deponents, is attested both by the Curé of Corps, and the Mayor of La Salette.

Peter Selme deposed, that "Maximin came to the Ablandins on the 14th of September, 1846. He went on that and the following days to guard four cows, in my property on the top of the mountain *aux Baisses*, a little distant from the summit, where the cross has recently been planted. The whole of the slope belonged to private proprietors. But the commune of La Salette possesses the property of the level, on which the events passed of which Maximin and Melanie speak. As I feared little Maximin might not be careful enough of the cows, since they might easily fall into one of the numerous ravines, I went and worked in that field, on Monday the 14th, Tuesday, Wednesday, and Friday of that week. I declare that during all these days I never lost the boy out of sight for an instant. It was easy to observe him from any part of my field, for no elevation of the ground intervened. I ought, however, to add that, on the first day I took him to the level of which I have spoken, and pointed out to him a little stream where he was to take the cows to drink. He took them there every day at midday, and immediately returned under my own eye. On Friday, the 18th, I saw him playing with little Melanie Mathieu, who guarded the cows of Bapiste Pra, my neighbor, whose farm joined mine. I know not whether the child was acquainted with her before he came to me, or whether or not he had made her acquaintance at the Ablandins. I never saw them together before. They both went very early in the morning to their fields, and did not return until night, when, after having their suppers they went to bed. On Saturday, the 19th, I returned to my field, as usual, with little Maximin. Towards eleven o' clock, or half-past eleven, in the morning, I told him to take the cows to the spring on the level, on the north side of the mountain. The child then said, 'I will go and call Melaine Mathieu, and we will go together.' On that day, he did not return to me in the field after taking the cows to drink. I only saw him again that night at the house, when he brought them back to the sheds. I then said to him: 'Why, Maximin, you didn't come back to me in the field,' 'Oh!' he said to me, 'you didn't know what has happened!' 'And what has happened?' I asked. He said, 'We found by the stream a Beautiful Lady, who amused us a long time, and talked to me and Melaine. I was afraid at first; I did not dare to fetch my bread which was by her, but she said to us: 'Fear not, my children; come near; I am here to tell you great news.' And the child then recited to me what he has so often repeated since to all who question him upon it. Next morning, I and my neighbor sent the two children to the Curé of La Salette, who, the same day at Mass, made known to his parishioners what they had seen and heard. This my neighbor told me, for I did not hear Mass at La Salette, but I took little Maximin to his father at Corps, as I had promised him to do. The child did not return again to our hamlet, where Melanie continued to remain until the month of December. He only passed through when he accompanied the numerous pilgrims who went to the Mountain. I further declare it to be my conviction that the children, in relating what they say they saw and heard, did not recite a lesson they have learnt. During the four days and a half that the little boy guarded my cows, and during which I never lost him out of sight, I never saw either priest or layman come near him or speak to him. Little Melanie went several times to guard cows in her master's field, whilst Maximin was with me. I saw her always alone, and if any one had come and spoken to her, I certainly should have seen it, for my field and Bapiste Pra's are one beside the other, on the same side of the mountain, and they have both a plain surface, and it is enough to stand up to see over and into every part of both of them. I ought to add, that on one of the days of the week Maximin guarded my cows in the field called Babou; he was not alone that day, but was watched, as on other days, either by my wife or myself."

This day appears to have been Thursday.

I need scarcely remind the reader that there are no hedges or fences on those mountains.

Baptiste Pra deposed, that "Melanie Mathieu entered my service in the month of May, 1846, and she remained in the hamlet of the Ablandins until the commencement of December of the same year. During the six days that Maximin Giraud of Corps guarded the cows of Peter Selme, my neighbor, I did not observe that these children were acquainted with each other. They might have met, either in my field, which joins that of Peter Selme, or whilst taking the cows to drink on the north of the mountain, at the *Baisses*. On Saturday, the 19th of September, 1846, they both came and told me what they had seen or heard on the level. Next morning they went together to the Curé of La

Salette, who the same day at Mass told it from the pulpit to his parishioners. Little Maximin the same day returned to Corps. He returned no more to our hamlet. Little Melanie remained, and she has been interrogated since then by a great number of persons. I ought to add, before signing, that for some days at first I did not believe the statement of the children, and I several times tried to induce little Melanie to take the money offered her to keep silence. The child constantly refused the money offered to her. She has always persisted, in spite of threats as well as promises of reward. The Mayor of La Salette, amongst others, tried in vain all sorts of means to put the child in contradiction with herself; he could not succeed. He then offered her money; she refused it, and she replied to his menaces, that she would always and everywhere repeat what the Blessed Virgin had said to her."

These depositions were signed the 27th of November, 1847. The Abbé Rousselot adds, from the notes of Mr. Lagier, that Maximin and Melanie could scarcely have seen each other at Corps; their parents lived at the opposite extremities of the town, and Melanie, before her service with Baptiste Pra, had been in service two years at Quet, and two years at St. Luce. The children have always asserted that they were not acquainted with each other until two days before the Apparition, and then saw each other but a short time. Indeed, Maximin could not have been more than six years old when Melanie, not eleven, left Corps and went to service. It must be observed that these children neither spoke nor understood much of the French language. Their own is a singular *patois*, having a resemblance to the Italian, and some affinity with the Spanish. Thus, they knew not the French for so common an object as the potato.

To give the characters of the two children more completely, I must anticipate a little. Several months after the great event of their lives, they were both placed at school, under the care of the respectable Superioress of the convent at Corps. After they had been there a year, the Superioress was called upon to give her opinion of them before a commission of enquiry appointed by the Bishop of Grenoble. She said:

"Maximin has but ordinary abilities; he is sufficiently obedient, but light, fond of play, and always in motion. He never speaks to us of the affair of La Salette, and we avoid the subject with him, that he may not take any importance to himself. After undergoing those long and frequent questionings to which he is subjected, he never tells us, or the other children, or any one, who it is that asks for him, or what questions have been put to him. After his visits to La Salette, and after his interrogations, he comes back as simple and as well behaved as if nothing had passed which concerned him. It is not my wish for him to receive the money which some pilgrims offer him. When by chance it has been forced upon him, he brings it faithfully to me, and in no way troubles himself whether I employ it for himself or for his parents. As to objects of piety, such as books, crosses, beads, etc., if he receives presents of them, he never cares to keep them. He often gives them away to the first companion he meets, and he often forgets or loses them, from the natural levity of his character. Maximin is not naturally inclined to piety; yet he likes to hear Mass, and willingly says his prayers when he is reminded of that duty. In a word, the child shows himself in no ways conscious that he is the object of the curiosity, the eagerness, the attention and caresses of such great numbers of people; he does not surmise that he is the primary cause of the prodigious concourse which takes place daily at La Salette."

Interrogated at a later period, the Superioress said: "During the past year Maximin, though taught almost every day, has not learnt to serve Mass well; nor has Melanie learnt to say well by heart the acts of Faith, Hope, and Charity, though I cause them to be taught her twice a day." Such are the two children by nature.

In my conversation with Maximin I asked him what he and Melanie had talked about on the day previous, and on the day itself, before the Apparition occurred, and if they talked about any religious subjects.

"No," he said, "they did not talk about anything religious; they did not talk much about anything — he amused himself."

"And how," I asked, "did you amuse yourself?"

"Chiefly," he replied, "by taking aim and pitching my knife into the turf."

I was struck with the same dark lustre, in the eyes of Maximin, when I first saw him, that I had observed in Melanie. They remind me of the effect of tropical climates. His eyes are prominent, his brows well marked, but somewhat depressed at the top of the arch. His forehead is clear, his general appearance is frank, and he prepossesses me favorably. His manner is free and easy, but still rustic. He answers readily when questioned, but his hands are restlessly employed about his knees. His voice has an independent drawl in it, and he has not an atom of mere human respect in his composition. All reports agree that he has made but a very poor way in learning; for he is both slow of mind, heedless, and volatile.

THE DISCOURSE

CHAPTER V

THE APPARITION

The 19th of September, 1846, fell on a Saturday. It was also the eve of the festival of our Lady of the Seven Dolors. Maximin and Melanie, conducting their cows, came down together from le Planeau upon the level, or terrace, called *Sous les Baisses*. The day was serene, the sky cloudless, the sun shone brilliantly. It was about mid-day, for they heard the distant sound of the Angelus bell. They took their provisions, and ate them by the side of a little spring, called *des hommes*, on the right of the little stream Sézia. When they had finished their repast, they descended, crossed the stream, and laid down their bags seperately, near the place where another spring sometimes flowed, but was at that time dry, though soon to become forever famous. They descended a few more paces, and then, contrary to their usual habits, as they afterwards said, they lay down at a little distance from each other and fell asleep. Melanie awoke first, and not seeing the cows, she awoke Maximin. They then crossed the stream together, ascended in a straight line to the opposite ground, and, on turning round, saw the cows lying on a gentle slope of Mount Gargas. They were about returning towards the dried-up spring to pick up their bags, but scarcely had they turned, when they saw a bright and dazzling light. Here we will give the recital of the children. We will give it exactly as they gave it on the same evening to their employers; as they gave it the next morning to the Curé of La Salette; as Melanie recounted it the same day to Monsieur Peytard, the Mayor of La Salette; as they gave it on the following days, Melanie to the inhabitants of La Salette, Maximin to the inhabitants of Corps, and as they have constantly given it to all enquiries ever since.

MELANIE'S RECITAL

"We fell asleep . . . then I woke first, and I did not see my cows. I woke Maximin. 'Maximin,' I said, 'quick, let us go and look for the cows.' We passed the little stream which went up straight before us, and saw the cows lying down on the other side; they were not far off. I was coming down first, and when I was five or six steps off the little stream, I saw a brightness like the sun, it was far more brilliant, but it had not the same color; and I said to Maximin, 'Come quick, and see the bright light down there'; and Maximin came down, saying, 'Where is it?' I pointed to it near the little spring, and he stopped when he saw it. Then we saw a *Lady* in the bright light; she was sitting with her head in her hands. We were afraid; I let my stick fall. Then Maximin said: 'Keep your stick; if *it* does anything I will give *it* a good knock.' Then the *Lady* rose up, crossed her arms, and said to us, 'Come near, my children, be not afraid, I am here to tell you great news.'

"Then we crossed the little stream; and she advanced to the place where we had been sleeping. She was between us both. She said to us weeping all the time that she spoke. (I clearly saw her tears falling):

" 'If my people will not submit, I shall be forced to let go the hand of my Son. It is so strong, so heavy, that I can no longer withold it.

" 'For how long a time do I suffer for you! If I would not have my Son abandon you, I am compelled to pray to Him without ceasing. And as to you, you take no heed of it.

" 'However much you pray, however much you do, you will never recompense the pains I have taken for you.

" 'Six days have I given you to labor, the seventh I have kept for myself, and they will not give it to me. It is this which makes the hand of my Son so heavy. Those who drive the carts cannot swear without introducing the name of my Son.

" 'These are the two things which make the hand of my Son so heavy. If the harvest is spoilt, it is all on your account. I gave you warning last year about the potatoes, but you did not heed it. On the contrary, when you found the potatoes spoilt, you swore, you took the name of my Son in vain. They will continue to decay, so that by Christmas there will be none left.' "

"And as I did not well understand what was meant by potatoes, I was going to ask Maximin what was meant by potatoes, and the Lady said to us:

" 'Ah! my children, you do not understand; I will say it in a different way.' Then she continued:

(Melanie continues the recital in the *patois* of the country.)

" 'If the potatoes are spoilt, it is all on your account. I gave you warning last year, but you would not take heed of it. On the contrary, when you found the potatoes spoilt, you swore, and introduced in your oaths the name of my Son. They will continue to decay, so that by Christmas there will be none left.

" 'If you have wheat it is no good to sow it; all that you sow the insects will eat. What comes up will fall into dust when you thrash it.

" 'There will come a great famine. Before the famine comes, the children under seven years of age will be seized with trembling, and will die in the hands of those who hold them; and others will do penance by the famine.

.   " 'The walnuts will become bad, the grapes will rot. If they are converted, the stones and rocks will change into loads of wheat, and the potatoes will be self-sown on the lands.

" 'Do you say your prayers well, my children?' Both of us answered: 'Not very well, Madam'.

" 'You must be sure to say them well, morning and evening. When you cannot do better, say at least an *Our Father* and a *Hail Mary*. But when you have time, say more.

" 'There are none who go to Mass but a few aged women, the rest work on Sunday all the summer; and in the winter, when they know not what to do, they go to Mass, only to mock at religion. During Lent they go to the shambles like dogs.

" 'Have you never seen wheat that is spoilt, my children?'

" 'Maximin replied: 'Oh! no, Madam'. For me, I did not know of which of us she asked this question; and I replied very gently: 'No, Madam, I have never seen any yet.' 'You must surely have seen it, you, my child (turning to Maximin), once when you were near the farm of Coin, with your father.

" 'The master of the field told your father to go and see his ruined wheat. You went both together. You took two or three of the ears into your hands and rubbed them, and they fell all into dust; and then you returned home. When you were still half an hour's distance from Corps, your father gave you a piece of bread, and said to you, 'Here, my child, eat some bread this year at least; I don't know who will eat any next year if the wheat goes on like that.' Maximin replied: 'Oh! yes, Madam, I recollect now; just this moment, I did not remember'."

"After this the Lady said to us 'Well, my children you will make this to be known to all my people.'

"She passed the little stream, and again said to us, 'Well, my children, you will make this to be known to all my people.' Then she ascended to the place where we had gone to look for our cows. She did not touch the grass. She moved along on the tips of the grass. I and Maximin followed her; I passed before the *Lady*, and Maximin a little on the side, two or three steps. And then the *Beautiful Lady* arose a little from the ground. (Melanie raised her hand a yard, or more, above the ground, by way of illustration), then she looked towards heaven, then towards the earth; then we saw her head no more, then her arms no more, then her feet no more; we saw nothing more but a brightness in the air; after this the brightness disappeared. And I said to Maximin: 'Perhaps it is a great saint'. And Maximin said to me: 'If we had known it was a great saint, we would have asked her to take us with her.' And I said to him: 'Oh that she were here still!' Then Maximin darted his hand out to catch a little of the brightness; but there was nothing there any more. And we looked well, to see if we could not see her. And I said: 'She will not let herself be seen, that we may not see where she goes.' Afterwards we looked after our cows."

At this point Melanie is asked: Did she tell you nothing else?

Melanie: No, Sir.

Q.   Did she not tell you a secret?

Melanie: Yes, Sir, but she has forbidden us to tell it.

Q.   What did she speak about?

Melanie: If I tell you what about, you will soon find out what it is.

Q.   When did she tell you your secret?

Melanie: After speaking of the walnuts and the grapes. But before giving it to me, it seemed to me that she spoke to Maximin, and I heard nothing.

Q.   How was she clothed?

Melanie: She had white shoes, with roses round them of all colors, a gold-colored apron, a white robe with pearls all over it, a white cape over her shoulders, with roses round it; a white cap, bent a little forwards; a crown with roses round her cap. She wore a very small chain, on which was hung a cross, with a figure of our Lord; on the right were pincers, on the left a hammer. At the extremities of the cross another large chain fell, like the roses round the cape. Her face was white and elongated. I could not look at her long together, because she dazzled us.

MAXIMIN'S RECITAL

"After we had given drink to our cows, and eaten our meal, we fell asleep beside the little stream, close by a little dried-up spring. Melanie awoke first, and she awoke me, to go and look after our cows. We went to look for our cows, and on turning around, we saw them lying on the other side of the mountain. Then, as we were coming down, Melanie saw a great brightness on towards the spring, and she said to me, 'Maximin, come and see this brightness.' I went towards Melanie, then we saw the brightness open, and within it we saw a *Lady* sitting like this (Maximin sits down, with his elbows on his knees, and his face in his hands,) and we were afraid. And Melanie said, 'O my God!' and she let her stick fall. And I said to her, 'Keep your stick; I will take care of mine; if *it* does anything to us I will give *it* a good knock.' And the Lady rose up, crossed her arms, and said to us:

"Come near, my children, fear not, I am here to tell you great news.'

"And we felt no more fear; then we went forward, and crossed the stream, and the *Lady* came towards us, for a few steps, from where she was seated, and she said to us:

"If my people will not submit, I am compelled to let go the arm of my Son," etc.

Here Maximin recounts the words of the *Lady* in nearly the same words as Melanie.

He then continues his recital.

"Then she crossed the little stream; and at two steps beyond the stream, she said:

"Well, my children, you will cause this to be known to my people."

"Then she ascended some fifteen paces, gliding over the herbage as if she were suspended and moved on by other hands; her feet only touched the top of the herbage. We followed her up the ascent. Melanie passed before the *Lady*, and I to one side, at a distance of two or three paces.

"Before she disappeared, this *Beautiful Lady* rose up like this (Maximin marks with his hands an elevation of about a yard and a half). She remained suspended thus in the air a moment, then we saw her head no more, then the arms no more, then the rest of the body no more; she seemed to melt away. And then there remained a great light which I tried to catch with my hands, as well as the flowers she had at her feet; but there was nothing there.

"And Melanie said to me, 'It must be a great saint.' And I said to her, 'If we had known it was a great saint, we could have asked her to take us with her.' Afterwards we felt great satisfaction, and we spoke of all we had seen, and then we looked after our cows. At night, when we had got home to our masters, I was a little sad; and as they asked what was the matter with me, I told them all that this *Lady* had said to me."

Q.   Tell me, Maximin, when did the *Lady* give you your secret?

Maximin: After she said, "The grapes will rot, and the walnuts will become bad." Then the *Lady* said something to me in French, and said, "You shall not say this, nor this, nor this." . . . She also kept silence for a short time; it seemed to me that she was speaking to Melanie.

Q.   What o' clock was it when you woke and saw the Lady?

Maximin: It was about two or three o' clock.

Such is the recital of Maximin. On the few discrepancies, in form rather than substance, between the narratives of the two children, I shall make some observations later on. It is the common remark of the mystic writers, that celestial apparitions cause dismay at first, but end in consolation; whilst those which are of an infernal origin, show whatever attractiveness they may put forth at the very beginning, but end in troubling the soul. And the recorded visions of the Sacred Scriptures bear out this rule. So far as this test is concerned, I leave the reader to apply it to the simple narrative of these uneducated children. One feature runs through the whole of this case, which as a proof of the sincerity of the children, has struck me much, and strikes me the more as I examine more minutely into it. In replying to those countless interrogations which have been put to them, of which whole volumes have been recorded, whilst they thought but of describing the apparition, and the circumstances attending their own share in it, they have unconsciously portrayed their own characters, in all their lights and shades, down to the minutest particles, and that with a truthfulness which nothing but the fact of their having so thought and so acted at the time, can explain. Nor can it be explained how they did so think, and act and speak, if they had not before them the appearance they describe, and had not heard what they say they heard. It was perhaps the instinct of this fact that led the *Times* to admit that the children were not the deceivers. Maximin was as restless as he always is. He was as free from, what we must call again, human respect. He kept to his stick. If *it* did anything, he would give *it* a good knock. He could not make the same efforts to look as Melanie. He took his hat off his head, and twirled it on his stick, and put it on again. With the end of his stick he sent the pebbles rolling about. Various thoughts passed through his head. He says he had heard talk of sorceresses, and he thought she might be a sorceress. Then, when the beautiful *Lady* spoke of the heavy arm of her son, he thought she meant that her Son had been beating her; for, as he at a later time explained, "he did not then know that the *Lady* was the Blessed Virgin." "Nay," as he said at another time, "though he knew there was a Blessed Virgin, yet he did not know at that time *who she was.*" Melanie, though almost as ill-instructed as Maximin, was more reflective, and had other thoughts. As stated to me by Maximin, the exact words in which, after the vision had departed, she found utterance, were these: "It is either God, or my father's Blessed Virgin, or a great saint." Maximin caught at the last words, his ideas were changed, and he regretted he had not asked the great saint to take them with her.

In reading the many conversations taken down from the lips of the children, or in conversing with them, it is very remarkable, as the Abbé Rousselot has also observed, how completely the whole form and presence of the *Beautiful Lady* is fixed and, as it were, stereotyped in their minds. Indeed, quite as much as her words. However new or unexpected the question, they are never at a loss; they never require time to remember; they seem to look for an instant, as if at the type within them, and then reply, both with clearness and confidence. And all their answers given, as they have been, to every rank and class of persons, questioning with every degree of ability, and under all possible varieties of circumstances, and that for a course of more than eight years, when brought together, are found to have a consistency, a keeping, and a symmetry, such, that the last replies tend only to add a finer perfection to the picture which they sketched on the first day. Thus, whilst the prophetic words stand in their original simplicity, unchanged and unadded to, this incessant agitation of inquiry has brought out a development in the description of the apparition. Then

the children have learnt the French language and have, with time and
the expansion of their minds, acquired an accumulation of ideas and
images, as instruments with which to convey more perfectly what has
always remained pictured within them, as it were with light on their
souls.

Criticism will remark upon the more spiritualized form which
the vision takes with these latter explanations; but then it should be
recollected, that whilst the words they heard were not their own, and
have no analogy with their characters, the descriptions of the vision
emanate from themselves; and at first their minds were rude, and their
own speech imperfect. The evidence upon which these descriptions
rest is derived more abundantly from Melanie than from Maximin.
She has naturally been more questioned on the subjects of appearance
and costume. She looked and observed more. The restlessness of
Maximin made him less endure the exceeding brightness, and hence
he could not look into the face of *the Lady*, but only saw the headdress
and the form from beneath the face. For, the face, he remarks, was too
dazzling for him to bear. Then, again, he was much the younger of the
two.

Both describe *the Lady* as unusually tall. Neither of them can
speak of the materials or of the texture of her costume. They describe
the light which they first saw, as incomparably brighter than the sun,
and when asked about its color, they say there is no color in the world
at all resembling it. In describing *the Lady*, the only ideas they can use
are those of form, light and color. Yet the colors, they say, are like no
earthly colors, for all is so brilliant, and yet one thing is described as
far more brilliant than another. Thus, the pearls which covered the
robe were *very* brilliant. The sleeves were deep, and covered the
hands, and were crossed over beneath the breast, so as partly to cover
the crucifix. The cross was "yellow, but bright"; the figure of our Lord
upon it was also "yellow, but far more bright". Lately, when the
Superior of the Mission of La Salette was preparing a statue representing the Apparition for the church, he went, as he told me, and asked

Maximin apart, if the figure of our Lord had a crown of thorns.
Maximin looked for a moment and said, "No." He then went and
asked Melanie. After an instant she answered "No." The pincers and
hammer were placed on the arms of the cross beyond the nailed hands.
When told there was no such thing as blue roses, Melanie answered
at once, "but there were blue roses, and roses of all colors." Yet they
declare that they were not roses, they were so bright. There were none
round the lower part of the dress, as sometimes pictured, but only
round the feet. The apron descended nearly, but not quite, down to the
length of the robe. Melanie speaks of spangles covering this apron, but
when spangles were produced, she said, "they are not like these, these
are not brilliant, these are poor." The greatest difficulty has been to
obtain a correct description of the head-dress. They use the word cap,
and even point to caps as worn by pilgrims from one of the provinces,
as having some resemblance to it in form. But when questioned more,
Melanie can give no idea of any other substance in it than light, as if
it were formed of streams of brilliancy. It bent forward at the top, and
was not quite pointed. Over the brow there was a diadem of roses, out
of which the cap arose. But in the center of each rose there was
something exceedingly full of light. She calls it a *magister*, by which
she always means something excessive in its brilliancy. And then a
fine thread, or ray of light, came out of those bright centers, which
enlarged itself as it lengthened. Then there went up and out of the
diadem, from between the roses, something like brilliant pearls,
"which made a branch, and then little branches". The *Lady* not only
glided over the herbage without pressing upon it but, in crossing the
little stream, she glided on one of the stones in the middle of it. No
representation which has been produced can give the children any
satisfaction. They say that nothing can give any notion of the beauty
or the brilliancy of the *Lady*. Then Melanie speaks of the gentle
sweetness of her voice as beyond all comparison. And Maximin says
of its sweetness, that all the finest symphonies of church choirs which
he has since heard, are nothing to that voice.

To complete this description, I will add a letter of Melanie's which was written last year.

"Monsieur,

"It is by command of our Mother Superioress that I do myself the honor of writing a few lines, to speak to you of MARY, our mother and our Protectress; but what shall I say? . . . I, who loved her so little before she showed herself to me on the privileged Mountain, and who yet love her so little! Alas! I am the most miserable of creatures! . . .

"I am desired to say something of OUR LADY OF LA SALETTE; but I can only repeat again what you have already seen in books; nevertheless I may be able to add some little particulars which perhaps are not written.

I.   The Blessed Virgin was surrounded by two most overwhelming brightnesses. I know not how to name the color of the first brightness, which was seen by us, and which extended for three or four yards around our Mother; and thus, in that light which was motionless, the two wretched little cowherds were enveloped: then there came forth from our good Mother another brightness, more beautiful and brilliant, which reached to us, and moved and formed rays. I could not look for long without my eyes filling with tears; yet at that time I felt myself stronger to support it; for, if all had not been supernatural, even at the approach of the first light, I should have been reduced to dust; and we were so near the Blessed Virgin that a person could not have passed between us.

II. The Blessed Virgin had roses round the cape over her shoulders, and round her shoes there were white, blue, and red roses; from the centers of the roses there came a sort of flame, which rose up like incense; and mingled with the light that surrounded our Protectress. In short, it is more than possible that God, without letting us know, had changed our eyes, so that we could remain so long a time, as it were, in a sun. At the moment that the Blessed

Virgin spoke, the sun we have on earth appeared but as a dim shadow; so I am not astonished that my eyes looked upon the sun, as if it were not so brilliant now as it seemed before the apparition.

III. Whilst the Blessed Virgin spoke to us she wept, and shed many tears. Oh, Monsieur, who would not weep at seeing their Mother weep? And yet our Mother weeps over the ingratitude of her children. The tears of our good Mother were brilliant; they did not fall on the earth, they disappeared like sparks of fire. The features of Mary were white and elongated; her eyes were very gentle; her look was so kind, so affable, and attracted one towards her in spite of oneself. Oh, yes, one must be dead not to love Mary! one must be more than that! one must never have existed not to love Mary! and not to cause her to be loved! Ah! . . . If I could make myself heard through all the universe, then I might content the desire I have to make Mary to be loved.

"Jesus and Mary, be ye known and loved by all hearts: this is always my first morning sigh when I awake.

"Have the great kindness, Monsieur, not to forget me in your prayers; and however unworthy, I will pray for you.

"Accept the homage of profound respect, with which I am, Monsieur, your very humble servant.

"Sister MARY OF THE CROSS,
"The least of Religious."

THE TWO WITNESSES – MAXIMIN AND MELANIE (In 1847)

CHAPTER VI

THE EVENTS AFTER THE APPARITION

The 20th of September, the day following the apparition, was Sunday. And early that morning the children were sent by their employers to tell their narratives to the Curé of the Parish. The Abbé Perrin, Curé of La Salette, was an aged and venerable ecclesiastic. At the parochial Mass he told it in his simplicity to his parishioners. Some who had heard it already from the children had declared it was the Blessed Virgin, and he drew the same conclusion. He made it the subject of his exhortation, and, mingling his tears with those of his people, he spoke of the anger of the Son of God against blasphemers, and against those who neglected the day of the Lord. This gave it publication. But no one suspected the good Curé of having devised a fable. He neither knew Maximin, who had been in his parish but five or six days, nor Melanie, who, for nine months she had been there, had seldom come to the church. He did not even know that part of the mountain; he had never had occasion to make the laborious ascent to a solitude where only those who kept cattle went during the day for a few months of the year. Ten days afterwards the Curé was removed for this act, and a young ecclesiastic of the same name, who was a stranger to the event, was substituted in his place. This is that Abbé Perrin whose name appears in the later investigations, and who is not to be confounded with his predecessor. He is a young man of considerable acquirements, and of very amiable manners.

The same morning the employer of Maximin took the boy home to his father at Corps, according to his promise, and thus, whilst Melanie was evangelizing the Apparition at La Salette, Maximin was doing the same thing at Corps. The father of Maximin would not believe. But when he heard what had been said by *the Lady* of the ruined wheat, and of her repeating his own remark to his son, when he gave him the bread, then he believed.

Those who went up the Mountain found the little dried-up spring flowing copiously. As the terrace was the common property of the "Commune" of La Salette, and all its inhabitants had the right to graze upon it, they were well acquainted with its pastures. Since that time the water has never ceased to flow; it is beautifully clear, and falls for the breadth of some three feet down the face of small rocks ranged in a semi-circle. The news spread rapidly, and put vast numbers of persons in motion towards the Mountain.

Within eighteen days of the event, the Bishop of the diocese had published a mandate to his clergy, enjoining them, under pain of suspension, to be incurred by the very fact, on no account to publish or encourage the supposition of a miraculous manifestation upon which the proper authority had not spoken. And thus for twenty months the clergy of the diocese remained silent, observing, indeed, and interrogating with the rest, but with their mouths absolutely sealed upon the subject. But there came in numbers, clergy from other dioceses, lawyers, physicians, and persons of every class, as well as the multitudes of the poor.

The children were continually subjected to examinations. They were taken to the place; they were interrogated apart; their statements were confronted; suspicions were attached first to this person, then to that, but without any grounds; no evidence would come up against them. So the children continued to be brow-beaten, coaxed, tempted with bribes, threatened and cross-questioned in every way that human ingenuity or practical skill could devise. The civil authorities even mingled threats of imprisonment with their interrogations, and the "brigadier de gendarmerie" produced cords, as if to bind Maximin. But no contradiction could be elicited, no signs of fraud could be brought out, nor could the children be silenced. They were to make the "great news" pass to all the people, they said; and they would rather die than neglect to do as they were told.

"But," it was asked of Melanie, "if the Blessed Virgin commanded you to tell this to all her people, you are not doing it, since you remain here (in the convent)?"

Melanie: I tell it to all who ask me.

Q.   Why did you not go and publish it in all the cities?

Melanie: I am not allowed to go.

Q.   If the Blessed Virgin commanded you would you go?

Melanie: I would go.

Q.   But if they were disposed to put you to death on this account, would you not be silent?

Melanie: Surely not! one could die but once; and after I was dead, I could never die more.

Q.   Do you like to speak of all this?

Melanie: It does not affect me.

Q.   Would you not rather speak of it?

Melanie: I should rather not, provided people knew it.

Among others came the venerable Bishop of La Rochelle (later on, Cardinal Villecourt.) This distinguished prelate made a journey of two hundered leagues to enquire and to converse with the children. On his return, he wrote to the Bishop of Grenoble: "I have come back with a conviction which scarcely differs from evidence." And within eight months of the event, he published the work, in which he narrated the history of his enquiries, and gave expression to his own private convictions. Miracles, through the instrumentality of the water of the fountain, began to be reported at a very early period, and as the cases increased in numbers, they began also to be enquired into.

On the first Anniversary of the Apparition, a most extraordinary and unlooked for spectacle took place on the Mountain. The anniversary occurred on a Sunday. It was anticipated that far greater than the usual number of pilgrims would come, and in order that the obligations of the Sunday might be satisfied, the Bishop allowed Mass to be said for the pilgrims. But, to the astonishment of everyone, no measure had been taken to invite or to draw persons together on the Mountain, they arrived from all parts of France, and even from other countries. Amongst them were two hundred and fifty clergymen. Though as yet there was neither habitation nor place of shelter, and the rain fell heavily from eight o'clock the night before until ten next morning, fifteen hundred persons passed the night on the Mountain. And by one in the morning, illuminating the darkness with torch-light, the head of a procession began to ascend the Mountain, whilst its farther extremities extended some twelve or fifteen miles along the roads in the direction of Gap and Grenoble, besides crowding the different paths of the mountain; and every hour of the morning poured some thousands of persons upon the scene of the Apparition. Two altars were erected, and covered over with sheds, and on these, the holy sacrifice was offered, some thirty or fifty times. Pressed together as this vast multitude was, yet by all accounts there was no disorder. Only four gendarmes were on the spot, and their sole occupation was to open the passage to the altars for the communicants, or to the fountain for those who came to drink of its waters. A thick cloud covered the mountain, and filled the valleys beneath, so that for a considerable time the pilgrims could only see the masses of human heads buried in the fog for the distance of a hundred paces from where they severally stood, though the whole breadth of the mountain resounded with pious canticles. At last the sun raised the cloud from the top of the mountain, and revealed the entire scene, whilst the stream of fresh arrivals were emerging out of the mists that still lay below. The *Magnificat* was chanted in two choirs by some thirty thousand voices. And then an ecclesiastic, tall of stature, and with stentorian voice, rose up above the multitude, and cried out over the vast assembly: "My brethren, let us pray for France." Then one common emotion united the hearts of all in one, and their prayers for their country were offered up with many tears. Mary had indeed called her people together through the voice of her young apostles. They were there, those two simple children, almost forgotten in the multitude. And it was only a year since they had been there alone, with Mary in their company. There has never been such another assemblage, though the anniversary has not once passed without calling together many thousands.

CHAPTER VII

EXAMINATION OF THE CHILDREN

As I write this book for Catholics, I have no occasion to prove that miracles and prophecies continue to be manifested in the Church of God. I will merely remark to any casual Protestant reader, that whilst this as a general principle is of Catholic faith, and, therefore, to be received by all Catholics, the particular instances in which this divine intervention is exercised, are left free for the examination and the criticism of the individual members of the Church, to be received and believed or not, according to the evidence. Yet there are certain of these manifestations of the Divine Goodness which, from the eminence of the authority which has pronounced upon them, from their universal acceptance, and from the piety and devotion which have grown out of them, acquire highest characteristics of *ecclesiastical* faith, and to call these lightly in question would be both rash and offensive to pious ears. The fact of La Salette has not attained to this high degree of authority. Though believed by vast numbers of Catholics on their private faith, it is still sifted and discussed by many others.

It is no argument against the acceptance of such a fact, that its recipients were mere children. We need not open the Paradisus Puerorum, to show that God has often chosen children as the instruments of His communications. The Sacred Scriptures give us the remarkable cases of Samuel and Daniel, each of whom was made a channel of prophecy at a tender age, and, as St. Benedict observes, "whilst young, judged the elders."

Poverty and the rudeness of an uncultivated nature is no disqualification; on the contrary, God chooses the weak and foolish things of this world, as St. Paul says, to confound the wise and strong. The Apostles themselves are the great instances of this economy.

The Prophet Amos was employed in the same occupation of a herdsman as the children of La Salette. And shepherds, guarding their flocks, were the first to whom was announced the "great news which should be to all the people," when the angels appeared to then in glorious lights, and sent them first, and before all mankind, to adore our Lord Incarnate in the arms of Mary.

La Salette is by no means the first sanctuary of Mary which has been founded through the instrumentality of children and shepherds. The sanctuary of our Lady of Calvary of Betharam, in the province of Béarn, so celebrated for the graces and favors received at its shrine, was erected because several shepherd children, whilst guarding their sheep on the mountain, had seen a *great light,* and discovered within it a beautiful image of our Lady.

In another instance a child, twelve years old, whilst seated near a fountain and guarding a flock of sheep, saw an apparition of Our Lady, who told him to admonish the Consuls of Mount Leon to build a church to her honor in that place. A church was built there, and became so famous for miracles that the sanctuary was called Notre Dame de Guérison, changed to *Garazon,* which signifies our Lady of Healing.

The famous sanctuary of our Lady of Montserrat was founded in 890 through a manifestation to shepherds whilst watching their flocks on the mountain. And the Pilgrimage of Our Lady of Valfleurie owes its origin to shepherds.

The best replies to the objections which have been raised to the fact of the Apparition have been furnished by the children themselves. Their replies to many of the interrogations, to which they have been subjected, have been carefully preserved. Simple and slow of mind in regard to all that is exterior to the subject of the Apparition, the children, when put on their defense, displayed such sagacity, brevity, and force, that their answers form one of the most wonderful and inexplicable circumstances of the entire case.

The Abbé Lagier was one of the earliest and most searching of their interrogators. He said to Melanie: You do not know French, you do not go to school; how could you recollect what the *Lady* said? She told you several times over? She taught you to remember it?

Melanie: Oh no; she told me but once, and I remembered it. And even if I did not understand it, those who know French understand it; that is sufficient.

Mlle. Des Brulais was on the most familiar and affectionate terms with Melanie. She asked:

Q.   Did you know French before the 19th of September, 1846?

Melanie: I did not know it.

Q.   Did you understand it?

Melanie: I did not understand it.

Q.   Did you immediately afterwards repeat in French what the Blessed Virgin told you in French?

Melanie: Yes, I said it as she said it to me.

Q.   You are very sure you repeated it in French, and not in *Patois*?

Melanie: I said in French what the Blessed Virgin said in French, and in *Patois* what she said in *Patois*.

Q.   You are very sure, quite sure, you did not say it in *Patois* the first day when you came from the mountain?

Melanie: How could I manage to say it in *Patois* when I could not say (or translate) it? I did not know French.

Q.   How could you repeat in French what the Blessed
                Virgin said in French, since you only knew the
                Patois?

Melanie: Well, I said it as she said it.

Q.   Do you know what you said?

Melanie: I said it as she had said.

Questions to Maximin: The *Lady* has deceived you, Maximin; she
                foretold to you a famine, and yet the harvest is
                everywhere good.

Maximin: How does that regard me? She told it to me; that
                concerns her.

Q.   The lady you saw is in prison at Grenoble.

Maximin: He will be very clever who catches her.

Q.   The *Lady* you saw was but a bright and luminous
                cloud.

Maximin: But a cloud does not speak.

Q. (A Priest): You are a little story teller; I do not believe you.

Maximin: How does that concern me? I am charged to say to
                you, not to make you believe it.

Another Priest: Come, I do not believe it: you are a story teller.

Maximin: Then why do you come so far to question me?

To Maximin (apart): But perhaps it was the devil who gave you this
                secret?

Maximin: No, for the devil has not our Lord on his breast,
                and the devil does not forbid a blasphemy.

Melanie: *(apart), in reply to the same question*: The devil
                may speak indeed, but I do not believe that it was

he, or that he can tell secrets like that. He would
not forbid swearing; he would not carry the cross;
and he would not tell us to go to Mass.

Melanie is examined by Mr. Rousselot, and about forty pilgrims, on the mountain, August, 1847. A Curé interrupted her narrative of the event: The *Lady* disappeared in a cloud?

Melanie :   There was no cloud.

The Curé insists: But it is easy to surround oneself with a cloud, and
          disappear.

Melanie: Then do you, Sir, surround yourself with a cloud,
          and disappear.

Melanie was examined on the anniversary of 1849: The Blessed
Virgin told you to cause it to be known to all the people. Whom do you
think to be meant by the people?

Melanie: Everybody.

Q.   Do you think, perhaps, that the angels are her
          people?

Melanie: Oh, Sir, the angels have no need of conversion.

Q.   In fact, this Lady whom you saw is in prison at
          Gap.

Melanie: No one but God can put her in prison. I should like
          to be in that prison.

Q.   However that may be, the things foretold by the
          Lady have not happened; there has been no fam-
          ine.

Melanie: Sir, the good God is not like men. He does not
          punish us directly.

To a similar objection (*we have seen no famine*), Melanie answered on another occasion: Sir, you are in great haste! And on another, the children replied: *But if the people do penance.*

Q.	Explain to me, Melanie, how it happened that the Blessed Virgin should have said, "*six days shalt thou labor,* I have reserved the seventh to *myself*"?
Melanie:	Ah, Sir, you are more learned than I, do you explain it.
Q.	What were you thinking of whilst the *Lady* spoke to you?
Melanie:	I listened.
Q.	Did she ask you if you said your prayers well?
Melanie:	Yes.
Q.	What did you answer?
Melanie:	We said, "*not very well, Madam.*"
Q.	What did the *Lady* say to you?
Melanie:	She said, "*you must say at least an* OUR FATHER *and a* HAIL MARY, *when you can do better you must say more.*"
Q.	That was very little, an *Our Father*, and a *Hail Mary*.
Melanie:	Sir, I did not know more, then; I did not even know that I ought to say as much.
Q.	If you were dying would you dare to say the same things?
Melanie:	Yes, Sir.

Q.	Would you not fear for the account you would have to give of this to God?
Melanie:	Oh, no, since I add nothing to it.

On the anniversary of 1849, after reciting his narrative, at the request of an English priest, Maximin said: Are you a Protestant, Sir?

Priest:	No, my little friend, I am a Catholic.
Maximin:	And yet you are English.
Priest:	Yes, but all the English are not Protestants, a good number are Catholics. Do you know what a Protestant is?
Maximin:	Yes, Sir, I know.
Q.	Are the Protestants Christians?
Maximin:	Oh, yes! they are Christians, but not Catholics.
Q.	What difference do you make between a Catholic and a Protestant?
Maximin:	The Protestants, then, don't go to confession, they will not have the Pope, and they will not believe in the Blessed Virgin.

Here Maximin's well-known prediction for being a missioner amongst savages came out; and the English Priest spoke to him of the great power of the English in so many distant countries, of their wars in China, etc., and he asked him if he should not be afraid if he saw the shells, such as had killed so many of the Chinese, falling in the midst of Corps. The child suddenly assumed a determined air, and turning to the Englishman, he said: Sir, the Blessed Virgin will not permit it; come now, neither the English, nor anybody, will come, and bombard *her* mountain.

Maximin has an impression that if, owing to the slowness of his studies and his little progress, he cannot be a priest, he will have to be a soldier. He says there are many good soldiers, and he will take care that his soldiers (for he does not dream of being in the ranks) shall neither blaspheme nor neglect the Sunday. In a recent conversation with his early spiritual father and kind friend, the arch-priest of Corps, he said: "I may, perhaps, get to be a priest at thirty, and if I am, I will have nothing but a shirt and soutane." The sense of a great and self-abandoned devotedness is deeply rooted in the souls of both these children. It is one of their most remarkable characteristics.

In September, 1847, Mlle. Des Brulais and Sister Clotilde were with Maximin in the convent of Corps. One of them said to him: You must be vexed, Maximin, when you see that they will not believe you speak the truth?

Maximin: Well, the Prophet Jonas did not say 'believe , or I will kill you'; he only said what God told him to say.

Q.   How, Maximin, do you think yourself like the Prophet Jonas?

Maximin: I am not *holy* like him; I am not *wise*, you see; but it is *the same thing*.

Q.   What! is it the same thing? you are very presumptuous, I think.

Maximin: Oh, yes! it is the same thing, only God had not His Mother then, and He sent the Prophet Jonas to Ninive; and as to me now, He sent His Mother to us, to tell us to *say it*; and we say it to all who wish it.

Q.   And who, my child, told you the history of the Prophet Jonas?

Maximin: Why, then, I read it in a chapter of the Bible.

Q.   But you know that the people say, that if the
                Blessed Virgin had chosen to speak to children,
                she would have selected wise ones?

Maximin: Ah, well! those others *were* perhaps no wiser.

The Abbé Albertin asked Maximin:

Q.   Do you not feel the weariness, my little fellow, of
                having to repeat the same thing every day?

Maximin: And you, Sir, do you feel the weariness of saying
                Mass every day?

Maximin interrogated September 19th, 1849:

Q.   Did they believe what you told when you came
                down from the Mountain?

Maximin: Very few believed; the rest laughed.

Q.   Who believed first?

Maximin: An old woman was the first, and she wept; and
                then in the morning the Curé believed it, and he
                wept.

Q.   Have you ever written your secret, Maximin?

Maximin: I have no need, Sir, it is written.

Q.   Ha! it is written, and where?

Maximin: *There*, Sir, (putting his hand to his heart), there is
                no need to write what is written.

Q.   But if you forget it?

                Maximin: Ah, well! God can make me remember
                it if He pleases.

Q.　　　　　　But if He does not please, it is lost?

Maximin:　　　How does that concern me? God can tell it to another, if He pleases.

Q.　　　　　　The famine has not come, Maximin; the Blessed Virgin did not say true then?

Maximin:　　　How do you know, Sir, that it will not come? The deluge was a hundred years coming after Noe said it.

Four days afterwards Melanie is examined very drily and minutely by a curé from Algiers.

Q.　　　　　　Can you say, I am sure that no water flowed then from the fountain, now called *miraculous*?

Melanie:　　　I am very sure, Sir, that none flowed before the Blessed Virgin had been seated there.

(Melanie retires and Maximin succeeds.)

Q.　　　　　　You are quite sure, Maximin, that no water flowed from the fountain near the cross of the Apparition before September 19, 1846?

Maximin:　　　Yes, Sir, I am very sure.

Q.　　　　　　How do you know it?

Maximin:　　　Why, Sir, I had just that very day led my cows to the little stream.

Q.　　　　　　How came there to be water in the stream and not in the fountain?

Maximin:　　　Why, Sir, the stream comes from higher up.

Q.　　　　　　So you saw the fountain flow after the *Lady* rose up?

Maximin:　　　I did not look, Sir, I saw nothing of it that day.

Q.   Why, then! when the *Lady* disappeared, did you
              not see the water flow? But still you ought to have
              seen it.

Maximin: Ah, no, Sir! since I did not even think of looking.

Q.   Who, then, did see it?

Maximin: People went up to La Salette on the Monday, and
              saw it; I went back to my father at Corps the day
              after.

Q.   And did you not go to see the fountain?

Maximin: Yes, Sir, I was there eight days after, with this
              person here, and we saw the fountain flowing.

I have room only for a few examples of the replies of the
Children when interrogated on their secret.

Melanie is asked:

Q.   The *Lady* gave you a secret, and forbade you to
              speak of it. Very well; but tell me at least if this
              secret concerns yourself or another?

Melanie: Whomever it concerns, I am forbidden to tell it.

Q.   Your secret is something you have to do?

Melanie: Whether it is something I have to do or not, I am
              forbidden to tell it.

The Abbé Chambon:

Q.   God has revealed your secret to a holy religious;
              but I had rather know it from you, and be sure that
              you do not deceive.

Maximin: If the Religious knows it she can tell it you; as for
              me I will not tell it.

Other persons put the following questions:

Q.	A time will come when you will tell your secret?
Maximin:	It will or it will not.

Q.	You ought to tell it to your confessor, from whom nothing should be concealed.
Maximin:	My secret is not a sin; in confession we are obliged to confess only our sins.

Q.   Suppose you should have to tell your secret or die?

Maximin (with firmness): I will die . . . I will not tell it.

M. *Gérente*, Chaplain of the Convent at Corenc:

Q.	I do not wish to ask your secret, Maximin, but this secret doubtless regards the glory of God and the salvation of souls. It ought to be known after your death. This, then, is what I advise you: Write your secret in a letter, and seal it; and let it be placed in the bureau of the Episcopal Residence. After the Bishop's death and your own, they will read this letter, and you will have kept your secret.
Maximin:	But some one may be tempted to open my letter . . . then again I don't know who goes to the Bishop's bureau.

Then, putting his hand first to his mouth, next to his heart, he added, with an expressive gesture:

My best bureau is there!

A priest of Grenoble said to Maximin:

You wish to be a priest; well, then, tell me your secret, and I will take care of you; I will write to the Bishop, and you shall go through your studies free of cost.

Maximin: If I must tell my secret to become a priest, I shall
                never be one.

In his celebrated letter, written after passing three days at La
Salette, Monseigneur Dupanloup, since made Bishop of Orléans, has
drawn up the argument from the character and replies of the children
with such a clearness, precision, and completeness, that I should do
injustice to my subject were I to substitute any reflection of my own
in its place. I will therefore give some extracts from this letter. After
giving sketches of the natural characteristics of the children, which
impressed him as disagreeable, his Lordship observes, speaking of
Maximin:

"And yet, every time this uncouth child is led back, however
suddenly, to speak of the great Event, there came a change over him,
strange, deep and instantaneous. And it is the same with the young
girl. The little boy retains the eyes and exterior which are so unpleasing;
but what was excessive in his uncouthness is at once lost. They
become of a sudden so grave, so serious; they assume involuntarily
something so singularly simple and ingenious, something even of
such respect for themselves, as well as for the subject they are
speaking of, that they inspire in those who listen to them, and impose
on their minds a sort of religious awe for the things they say, and a sort
of respect for their persons. I experienced these impressions constantly, and at times very vividly, and yet without ceasing to consider
them very disagreeable children.

"A remark occurs here, which has reference to what I have been
observing. When they speak of the great Event of which they profess
to have been witnesses, or when they answer the questions put to them
about it, this respect for what they say goes so far, that when they come
to make one of those truly astonishing and completely unexpected
answers, which confound their interrogators, cut short all indiscreet
questions, and resolve the gravest difficulties, simply, profoundly,

absolutely, they manifest no triumph whatsoever. One is astonished at times; as for them, they remain impassible. Not the slightest smile is seen to stir on their lips.

"Moreover, they never answer the questions addressed to them, but in the simplest and briefest manner. The simplicity of their replies is sometimes rustic, but their justness and precision is always extraordinary. The moment there is question of the great Event, they cease to show the ordinary faults of their age; above all, they are not idle chatterers. Maximin chats a good deal at other times, and when at his ease, he is a regular little gossip. In the fourteen hours we passed together, he gave me every possible proof of this defect; he spoke about everything that came uppermost with abundance of words, questioned me without restraint, gave me his opinion first, and contradicted mine. But with respect to the great Event which he relates, or his own impressions, his hopes or his fears for the future, or whatever attaches to the Apparition, he is no more the same child. On this point he never takes the lead, or commits an impropriety.

"He never gives a single detail beyond the precise question. When he has told the fact he is required to tell, or answered the question put to him, he is silent. One is eager, and would have him speak on, and add detail to detail, and tell all that he has experienced or continues to experience; but no — he adds not a word beyond the necessary answer. Then he quickly resumes the interrupted thread of conversation, speaks very freely of other things if they arise, or goes away.

"The fact is certain that neither one nor the other has any desire whatever to speak of the event which has made them so celebrated.

"According to all the information, which I gathered in the neighborhood, they never talk uselessly about it with any person, neither with their young companions, nor with the Religious who educate them, nor with strangers. When they are questioned, they answer; they simply tell the fact, if it is on a fact they are questioned; they simply give a solution, if it is a difficulty which is proposed to them; they neither add nor retrench beyond necessity. Whilst they never refuse to answer the questions put to them, no one has ever succeeded in inducing them to speak beyond a certain measure. You may multiply indiscreet questions, they never give an indiscreet answer. Discretion, that most difficult of virtues, is natural to them to a degree unheard of, but it is on this point only. Press them as much as you please, you find in them something invincible, which they cannot explain to themselves, which beats down all attacks, and involuntarily and securely plays with the strongest and most trying temptations.

"Whoever is well acquainted with children, and has studied their nature, light, unsteady, vain, talkative, indiscreet, and prying as it is, and will make the same experiments, that I have done, must share in the wonder and astonishment I have felt, and will ask himself, whether it be by the two children that he is baffled, or by some power which is superior and divine.

"I will add, that during the past two years the two children and their parents have remained as poor as before. This is a fact which I have verified sufficiently for my own satisfaction, and which it is most easy to prove beyond a doubt.

"I will set down here one observation which I have made, and it is this: that the two children, and more particularly Maximin whom I have seen both nearer and for a longer time, seem to have retained a simplicity and a spirit of humility so absolute, despite the honor they have received, and the renown with which this honor surrounds them, that this simplicity and this humility do not appear as if they had the characters of virtue in them in any degree whatsoever; they are as I have described, but with the air of not being able to be otherwise; and they are all this with a kind of passive naiveté, which even astounds, when one looks near and reflects upon it.

"The fact is, that they do not even understand the honors which they have received, and seem to have no idea of the interest which attaches to their names. They have seen thousands of pilgrims, 60,000 in one day, come in consequence of their story on the Mountain of La Salette. They have given themselves no airs of importance whatsoever, in consequence, nor have they shown any assumption either in their speech or manners. They regard all this without any astonishment, without a thought, without a return upon themselves. And, in fact, if what they say be true, they look on their mission in the same light in which the Blessed Virgin herself regarded it. She did not design to do them an honor; she merely designed to choose for herself witnesses who should be above all suspicion, through a simplicity so profound, so entire, and so extraordinary, that nothing could be comparable to it, and such as by course of nature could neither be explained nor understood; and she succeeded in her choice.

"Such is the first mark of truth which I discover in these children.

"*2nd. The second mark I find in the numerous replies, altogether above their age and capacity, which they have made off-hand in the different interrogatories to which they have been subjected.*

"For it must be remarked, that never in a court of justice have culprits been so harassed with questions about the crime with which they were charged, as these two poor little peasant children have been for the two years past on the matter of the vision which they narrate. Difficulties often prepared beforehand, sometimes for a long time, and insidiously planned, have always received from them prompt, brief, clear, precise, and peremptory answers. It is palpable that they would be absolutely incapable of such presence of mind if what they say were not true. They have been led like malefactors to the very spot of the Apparition, or of the imposture, if imposture it be, and neither have they been disconcerted by the presence of the most distinguished persons, nor frightened by menaces or abuse, nor seduced by coaxing and caressing, nor fatigued by the longest examinations; moreover, the frequent repetition of these trials has never caused them to contradict either themselves or each other. No two human beings could have less the air of being accomplices in a fraud; and were they really such, they must have a genius beyond example to be thus constantly coherent with themselves during the two years which have witnessed the continuance, without interruption, of this strange and rigorous trial. And yet with all this consistency they mingle the oddest contrasts; sometimes it is the rudeness of their origin which shows itself; at others it is impatience and a certain ill-humor; sometimes it is their gentleness, their calmness, and an imperturbable self-posses-sion; sometimes, or rather always, it is a discretion, a reserve, an impenetrableness to all persons alike — to parents, to companions, to acquaintances, to the entire universe.

* * *

"3rd. I have not been able to keep myself from acknowledging the fidelity with which they have kept the secret they profess to have received, a third characteristic sign of truth.

"They are two; each possessed of a secret, and that for nearly two years past. Each having a distinct secret, never has the one boasted of knowing that of the other. Their parents, their masters, their clergy, their companions, and thousands of pilgrims, have interrogated them about this secret and have asked of them some sort of revelation of it: to this end unexampled efforts have been made; but neither reasons of friendship, or self-interest, or promises, or threats, or the civil or ecclesiastical authority, (in 1851 the secrets were submitted by the children in writing to Pope Pius IX at his request) nothing has in any way been able to gain upon them in any degree; and now, after two years of continual efforts, nothing is known, absolutely nothing.

"I myself made the greatest attempts to penetrate into this secret.

* * *

"Such is the third mark of truth which I have observed in these children. And now, what is to be thought of it all? Is it truth, error, or imposture?

"All this cannot be explained reasonably but by one of the four following suppositions:

"1.   Either the supernatural truth of the Apparition of the story, and the secret of the children must be admitted. But this is attended with very grave and serious consequences; for if there be a deception, and it should some day be discovered, whether put in practise by these children, or by others, how many religious hearts will not feel that their sincerity has been wounded?

"2.   Or they have been deceived, and are still the victims of some hallucination. But whoever has made the journey to La Salette, and has examined everything, will not hesitate to affirm that this supposition is absolutely ridiculous and inadmissible.

"3.   Or the children are inventors of the fable, having concocted it themselves, and maintained it alone for now two years against everybody, without ever contradicting themselves. For my part I cannot for a moment admit this third supposition. The fable would appear more astonishing to me than the truth.

"4.   Or suppose, in fine, that there has been some contriver of all this, an impostor concealed behind the children, and that they have lent themselves to play the character which he has prepared for them, and which he teaches them each day to play anew. Without going to the bottom of this question, as M. Rousselot has done, I will merely answer that everything that precedes is repugnant to this suppositon. The inventor, as it seems to me, would have been at one and the same time the most *unskilful* in selecting for agents and witnesses of an imposture so extraordinary such beings as these are, and yet the most *skilful* in teaching them nevertheless successfully how to sustain such a part for two years before two or three hundred thousand spectators, observers, investigators, questioners of all kinds, without their having committed themselves in any thing at any one time, without any one having discovered the impostor behind the scenes, without a single indiscretion on the part of the children which could cause any one to be suspected, and without any mark whatever of fraud having appeared up to this time.

"There is nothing, then, to be received but the first supposition, namely, the supernatural truth of the whole, which, moreover, is very strongly confirmed ——

"1st. By the character which the children have each maintained unchanged.

"2nd. By the answers, altogether beyond their age and capacity which they have made in the different interrogatories to which they have been submitted.

"3rd. By the extraordinary fidelity, with which they keep the secret which they say has been confided to them.

"If I were under an obligation of pronouncing on this revelation, and saying 'yes', or 'no', and had to be judged on the subject in the rigorous sincerity of my conscience, I would say 'yes' rather than 'no'; Human and Christian prudence would compel me to say 'yes' rather than 'no'; and I do not think that I should have to fear being condemned at the judgment of God as guilty of imprudence and precipitation.

"Yours ever,
Dupanloup

" . . . , June 11, 1848.

After this beautiful analysis to which the extracts I have given from the examination of the children serve as illustrations, there is nothing left to be said on this part of the subject. I myself examined the two children, carefully studied their deportment, took the opinions of those who knew them best through constant intercourse, and confronted the different statements I received; and can attest, that, though it is now six years since these portraits of the two children were drawn by the Bishp of Orléans, after this long period they are as applicable as when they were drawn, with the exception of such changes as a little education may have accomplished in them. The basis of their characters remains unaltered. It is astonishing to find Maximin still the child he is here portrayed. (See Appendix - Note C.)

INTERIOR OF THE BASILICA

CHAPTER VIII

THE PROPHECY

A few discrepancies are found to exist between the words of the prophecy as severally narrated by Maximin and by Melanie. Thus, where Melanie speaks of the "*hand of my son*", Maximin says, "*the arm of my son*". Melanie speaks of "*the potatoes*"; Maximin uses the phrase, "*the potato crop*". But the variations are verbal, and fall most commonly on the particles, without at all changing the sense. Much greater discrepancies exist in the Gospel repetitions of our Lord's words by the different Evangelists. And if in the Gospels, whilst the substance and the sense remain identical, these verbal discrepancies are taken as an argument in proof of absense of collusion, the same argument holds good with respect to the narrative of La Salette.

It is a common characteristic of many prophecies of the Sacred Scripture, as of other prophecies, that they contain two elements, one of which is referable to an epoch distinct from the other. The prophet receives a first and a second revelation at one and the same time. The one refers to events near at hand, but often of comparatively less importance, except that it conveys immediate proof of its divine origin through the accomplishment of the event, and gives warning to those under whose eyes the events may fall. The other portion of the prophecy is more obscure, more secret, or more distant from the time of its fulfilment.

The first prediction of La Salette regarded the potato crop. Then the grapes were to rot. Then the walnuts were to grow bad. The general failure of the potatoes is a fact but too well known. But at Christmas there were to be none left. And it is an authentic fact that, in that part of the country there was not a potato left that could be eaten. In the winter of that year the people of those mountains were dying of hunger. "Fifteen days before Christmas," said her simple-hearted guide to the authoress of the *Echo of La Salette*, "there was not a potato to eat; you could not get for three francs what now (September 1847) you can get for eight sous." The Religious Sisters of Corps had their meal prepared with every particle of the bran in it, that they might have more to give to the famished people.

The writer just mentioned went one day in 1849, to a baker's at Corps to buy bread. It was on a Saturday. "Do you bake tomorrow?" she asked. "No, madam," he replied, " the ovens are not open here on Sunday since the Apparition; our Lady has forbidden us." "I had forgotten it was Sunday," she replied. "We do not want famine to come back again."

The failure of the vines, at that time not dreamed of, is now a matter of history. And in that district there are still many vines in a very bad state. Of the failure of the walnuts, an important crop for the people, I was myself witness this very year. Then a *"famine will come"*. But the time is not specified. God is not like men, to hasten punishment, as Melanie observes. And this prediction, like that of Ninive, "In forty days Ninive shall be destroyed," in however decisive terms it was uttered, seems in a latter part of the prophecy to be made contingent on the impenitence of the people.

"Children under seven years will be seized with a trembling, and will die in the arms of those who hold them." This prediction, again, seems to be put under similar conditions with the famine, *"if the people are converted"*. It is a fact that there was, soon after the event we are describing, a very unusual mortality amongst children in that portion of France. Enough of all these predictions occurred to give the people a warning of what might come. They looked on it in this light. A vast conversion has taken place. Swearing has ceased amongst those mountaineers, and Sunday is observed to a very great extent. There is a very great religious change in all the South of France, and

the pilgrimage to La Salette has been a main instrument of this conversion. The Bishop of Grenoble accidently mentioned to me that in the parish of which he had made the visitation the day before we met, there was not a *man* who had not made his Easter communion. There is at this moment a great movement in France, through associations, and in other ways, to bring a general observance of the Sunday. The good effect thus produced was noticed in a Protestant newspaper, the Record, though attributing its origin to an imposture. There are, also, widely spread societies for opposing blasphemy, and atoning for its commission. These movements have, in a great measure, flowed from the warnings of our Lady of La Salette.

We must expect to find prophecy couched in prophetic language. The language of God is not the language of man. Our Lord Himself becomes strong in His language, and almost seems to exaggerate in His vehemance, when He utters His woes on the Pharisees, or foretells the calamities of Jerusalem. But was the strongest language of God, by His prophets, either an exaggeration in itself or even a vehement figure? A partial conversion modifies the prediction in the event; or as at Ninive, there is an entire conversion, and the prediction is not fulfilled. But at Jerusalem there was a thorough impenitence of the Jews and the terrible prediction of our Lord was fulfilled to the very letter.

The prophecy of La Salette has the strong, plain energy and even the rhythm of the ancient prophets. Where did these children find this singular language, and how did their minds fall upon so strange a combination of incidents? Its very *unnaturalness* has been made one of the main grounds of objection, whilst in reality it furnishes a confirmation of its supernatural origin.

"If you have wheat, it is no good to sow it; all that you sow the insects will eat. What comes up will fall into dust when you thrash it."

It may here be objected that it is against all the laws of wisdom and prudence to exhort men to refrain from sowing the earth. But this is one of those energetic expressions of which the Sacred Scriptures abound in examples. Its object is to strike the hearer with a vivid sense of the uselessness of toiling and making sacrifices in opposition to the determinations of the Almighty. In a similar way our Lord warns those who shall have to encounter the desolation which He predicted to Jerusalem: "*He who is on the house-top, let him not come down to take anything out of his house. And he who is in the field, let him not go back to take his coat.*" And in the Book of Leviticus the Almighty gives this warning to His people: "*if you will not hear me, nor do my commandments, if you despise my laws, and condemn my judgments, I will quickly visit you with poverty and burning heat and consume your lives.* **You shall sow your seeds in vain**, *which shall be devoured by your enemies. But if you will not for all this obey me, I will chastise you seven times more for your sins.* **Your labor shall be spent in vain;** *the ground shall not bring forth her increase, nor the trees yield their fruit.*"

The sense of our Lady's words is this, and they are as full of charity as of terror; if you will not be converted, at least believe my words. Throw not away your wheat to perish, you will need every grain of it, for God will not let the soil produce more.

"*There shall come a famine, but before the famine, children under seven years shall be seized with a trembling, and shall die in the arms of those who hold them* .... **But if they are converted**, *the stones and the rocks shall be changed into heaps of wheat; and the potatoes shall be self sown in the lands!*" All then depends upon conversion or impenitence. A general and complete conversion will bring with it a wonderful abundance. Let any one observe the nature of cultivation in a mountainous country like Dauphiné, and they will better understand the literal sense of these words. A more extensive cultivation implies its spread over a higher range of stony and rocky heights. And the rocks and stones are literally reduced to soil, and changed into wheat. And where potatoes are abundant to excess, they will be imperfectly gathered, and will remain self-sown. The Almighty spoke of the promised land as "flowing with milk and honey". He promised, if His people observed His laws, that "the seed time should lay hold of the harvest". And the Psalmist says, "He brought oil from the hardest rock."

An objection was raised in the conferences at Grenoble, which must be treated here somewhat at length. In some manuscript copies of the recital of the Children, it was found that after the words: "*And in the winter when they know not what to do, they go to Mass only to mock at religion*," these words were found introduced, "*The boys put stones and other missiles in their pockets to throw at the young women.*" And several witnesses attested the introduction of these words. This interpolation was traced to Maximin. Melanie has never spoken of it. And Maximin had been asked by various persons why he had ceased to use it. And when further asked if he had never introduced such new expressions, he answered "*no*". Upon this difficulty it is to be remarked:

1st. That Maximin had never introduced the interpolated words in any of his earliest recitals. And that four months after the Apparition, when M. Lagier visited Corps, he had ceased to use them.

2nd. The first time that Melanie heard him use these words, she exclaimed, "What are you saying there? Did the Blessed Virgin say anything about that?"

3rd. It is an admitted fact that the practice described in these words prevailed at the time in Corps and some other parishes, so that the words were true in themselves as a description of the fact.

4th. It is clear that so far from being a contradiction of the text, these words are but an application of it to a specific and recognized state of things. They are an exemplification of its sense; a sort of paraphrase which brought it home to the hearers, and led to a correction of the abuse.

5th. When Maximin was examined on this point before the Ecclesiastical commission, he gave a two-fold answer. His first was that when he thus recited the passage, he was more occupied with the thoughts and the image of the Blessed Virgin than with her words. His second answer was that he heard many comments and applications of this part of his recital, and was led to ratify such comments by a simple "*yes*".

This last answer derives force from his replies to certain questions put by M. Rousselot before the Commission.

Q. Has it not been said that you mingled things in your recital which the Blessed Virgin never said?

Maximin: Yes, Sir. In a company of women and girls, they would have it out of me that the Blessed Virgin had spoken of dances and of bad confessions.

Q. Well; and so what did you answer these women?

Maximin: I told them that the Blessed Virgin did not say that, and as they would absolutely have it that the Blessed Virgin had spoken of these things, I said, as I left them to themselves, *have it just as you like.*

These explanations, if we bear in mind Maximin's habitual way of cutting short importunate and troublesome questionings, will show sufficiently how the words under consideration may have got inserted into some repetitions of his narrative. Still it will not explain how he himself introduced them when called to account for it by Melanie, though it may show how they got inserted into his own mind, and became there associated with the text.

I confess I am not satisfied with the Abbé Rousselot's solution of this part of the objection. I think that Maximin may be more satisfactorily cleared of the charge of wilful and deliberate falsification. Let me first observe that the sentence in question neither adds to the prophecy nor takes from it; nor does it add to or take from the sense of the Blessed Virgin's words irrespective of prophecy. It simply points to one of the recognized facts included in those abuses of the Sunday which her words denounce. And I need scarcely allude to that widely-received theory which maintains that even the prophets and apostles, when they record exterior, sensible and obvious facts amidst their revelations, do not receive such facts from direct inspiration, but are simply preserved from error in narrating them. Nor need I cite Gerson (Gerson De Examinatione Doctrinarum Part 1, Consid .í.), Benedict XIV (Bened. XIV. De Servor, Dei Beatif. et Canoniz. L. 3 c44; c. 47, c.53), or Amort (Amorat de Revelationibus. Cap. 22, s 1, Regula 33.), or the list of authorities he quotes, to show that true revelations, even revelations approved by the Church, are not always without some mixture in their narration of things unrevealed, or even untrue, so it be in a manner that does not affect the sense and bearing of the revelation itself.

And now, what is the case of Maximin? He often hears repeated a popular application of a part of his revelation, or he sees it himself, and it is quite obvious to every other person. It becomes associated in his mind with the words of that portion of his revelation, it signalizes a known abuse, and on one or a few occasions, thinking at the time, as he says, "more of the thoughts and the image of the Blessed Virgin than of her words," he introduces it into his narrative. But no sooner is he asked by his fellow-witness, if that is a part of the discourse of the Blessed Virgin, than he not only does not affirm that it is, but he ceases to use it. And when at a later time he is asked if he ever added to the words of the Blessed Virgin, he answers, "No". For he had no intention of adding these words as an imposition, and as a part of the Blessed Virgin's discourse. And this answer is in perfect keeping with the whole of his peculiar style and idiom, as any one may observe who has studied its character. It is just a little trait of that spirit of preaching for which at this early period he was athirst. The Superioress of the convent where he was at school, says of him at that period, that had he been allowed the liberty, he would have done very foolish things through his zeal. He could scarcely speak in French, and yet he wanted to mount the pulpit and preach. And next he would go to the neighboring town of Mens and convert the Protestants who are residing there. He would say:

"Let me go! let me go and convert them all!"

Q. But what will you say to them?

Maximin: I will say; Do as I do! Do as I do!

"Oh well then," replied his friend in raillery, "you will say: Be fond of play, as I am; be thoughtless, as I am; be indolent, as I am. For all this I certainly am."

Maximin: Say on; say on; and I will say: If they do no worse than I do, they will not sin so very much.

An exception has been taken to the vulgarity of the words, "*they go to the shambles in Lent like dogs.*" But the objector forgets our Lord's words to the Chananean, "It is not fit to take the bread of the children, and cast it to the dogs," or that stronger expression of St. Peter, "The dog has returned to his vomit."

There is one objection more which is made to the form of the prophecy. Why did Mary say, in the first person, "*Six days have I given you to labor in, the seventh I have reserved for myself, and you will not give it to me*"? The objection implies the answer. It supposes the objector to understand that this is the commandment of God and not of Mary. No one ever took it in any other sense. It is a quotation made in the words of the third commandment. When the Prophets declare the will of God, do they never speak in the first person? If any one in earnest had ever taken this for a commandment of the Blessed Virgin, there would have been reason in the objection. But it is too ancient, and too well known a formulary, ever to be mistaken. Hence preachers speak in this style; and had these very words occurred, as they stand, in a sermon, it would have attracted no observation.

There is one question more, and it awakes a sublime consideration. Why did the Blessed Virgin come and deliver this prophecy? Ah!
Why?

Maximin said, "God had no Mother when He sent Jonas, the
Prophet, to speak to the Ninevites. But to us He sent the Blessed Virgin
to bid us to say it to all his people."

Who does not know that there is a ministry in heaven as well as
on earth, and that "God has disposed the ministry of angels and men
in wonderful order," so that "they who serve Him in heaven succor and
defend us here on earth?"

Are we, then, who have greater helpers, in worse condition than
the Jews, who, to the latest period of their Church, had visions to
console, and prophecies to warn them? They forgot God, but they
remembered their Prophets and defenders with a certain lingering
veneration. So God sent them a vision of the Archangel Michael, or
of the Prophet Jeremias, or He sent them a new Elias, who might recall
the first to their mind. And our Lord appeared with Moses and Elias
by His side.

It seems as if, when they had ceased to hear Him, He sent those
who were nearer to their nature, whom they still loved, and were
inclined to listen to.

And thus in these latter days, when faith had grown faint, and
charity cold, among a people who had practically forgotten their God,
while still retaining a lingering child's love for their Mother, God
seized them by their last divine affection. God seems to say within the
depth of His infinite mercy: "They hear me no more. The voice of my
Son comes not to them. The Church they have ceased to know. My
day is to them as other days; and their blasphemies have turned my
wrath against them. Is there not one way of mercy left? Or shall this

people perish in their wilfulness? Perhaps they will listen to their mother. I will try them by their love for her. I will try them by her love for them. Perhaps she will bring them back to me, and again they may be my people."

And who that studies God's ways sees not how, as error thickens, and the devil gains power, his adversary, THE WOMAN, extends her power more and more within the Church of God? As those visions of her by St. John approach their consummation clothed with the sun, and with the moon beneath her feet, she is still in labor for the Church of Her Divine Son. And so she appears to us, from those Alps, with her crucified Son on her breast, pleading His cause, declaring His anger, warning us of the uselessness of her prayers without our own conversion, and weeping celestial tears. She urges us by a mother's love, and by all the sufferings and long patience of her Son. And she points to the two great causes which estrange us from God beyond a remedy, blasphemy, repelling Him from us; the neglect of His day, keeping us away from the reception of the graces which bring back the soul to him. When we have abandoned the ministry of the Church, the ministry of heaven alone remains. We have no right to it, but God is infinitely merciful, and our Mother is full of power with God, and full of tenderness and love for her children. (See Appendix - Note D.)

CHAPTER IX

THE SECRETS

The *Beautiful Lady* confided to each of the children a secret, and while the secret was confided to one, the other heard nothing, but only saw the movement of her lips. The secret was given to Maximin first and then to Melanie.

After the Apparition had disappeared, Maximin said to Melanie: "Why, she was a long time speaking to you, I only saw her lips move, but what did she say?" To which Melanie replied: "She told me something; but I will not tell you what; she has forbidden me." Maximin quickly replied: "Ah, I am well satisfied, Melanie; come, she told me something also; but I will no more tell you than you will tell me."

Towards the end of March, 1851, the Bishop of Grenoble learnt through the Cardinal Archbishop of Lyons, that His Holiness had intimated some desire to know these secrets. The prelate directed his secretary, the Abbé Auvergne, and the Abbé Rousselot, to instruct the children on their obligations, should the Pope, at a later period, give them an order to confide their secrets to him. The two ecclesiastics chose different times for seeing the children and each saw the one seperately from the other.

M. Auvergne went to Maximin at the Petit Séminaire, and taking him apart, he said to him: "Maximin, I am come to speak to you on something important. You promise me not to repeat what I am going to say?"

Maximin: Yes, Sir.

Q.   Do you believe that the Church has a right to

	examine and judge of all religious facts, apparitions, visions, etc.?
Maximin:	Yes, Sir.
Q.	That she may judge of these facts, is she not under an obligation to inform herself of the circumstances which accompany them?
Maximin:	Yes, Sir.
Q.	Can the Church be deceived?
Maximin:	No, Sir.
Q.	The Pope, the Vicar of Jesus Christ, can be deceived?
Maximin:	No, Sir.
Q.	If, then, the Pope asks your secret of you, you will tell it, will you not?
Maximin:	I am not yet before the Pope; when I am I will see.
Q.	How will you see?
Maximin:	According as he speaks to me, and I speak to him.
Q.	If he commands you to tell your secret, will you not tell it to him?
Maximin:	If he commands me I will tell it.
Q.	Have you any knowledge at what time you ought to tell it?
Maximin:	When I am made to tell it, it will then be known if I ought to have told it earlier or later, because my secrets — they are things that *ought to be* . . . here the boy stopped short . . . *known*, added his interrogator; Maximin added, "*Yes*".

The same day the Abbé Auvergne went to Corenc, to the convent in which Melanie was then placed. She answered the first question in much the same way as Maximin had done.

At the fifth question she was asked — if the Pope asks your secret of you, you will tell it to him, will you not?

She answered timidly, I don't know, Sir.

Q.   How is it you don't know? Would the Pope be mistaken, then, and ask you what he ought not to ask?

Melanie: The Blessed Virgin forbade me to tell it.

Q.   How do you know that it is the Blessed Virgin? The Church alone can know and say, and we must obey the Church.

Melanie: If it was not the Blessed Virgin, she would not have risen up in the air.

Q.   The devil may do that, and natural causes may have a like effect. The Church alone can distinguish between truth and error.

Melanie: Well, then, let it be declared that it was not the Blessed Virgin.

Q.   To know the truth, the Church has need to know your secret. You will tell it, Melanie, if the Pope commands you, will you not?

Melanie: I will tell it to him and *only* to him.

In the rest of the interview, the Abbé Auvergne strove in vain to induce her to tell her secret to some Bishop, Archbishop, or Prince of the Church. Melanie remained inflexible, and troubled. She ceased to give any other answer than the words, *I do not know*, words which she repeated some twenty times. She retired in sadness, and cried all the time of Vespers, at which she had soon after to assist.

M. Auvergne sent for her a second time.

Q.	Well, Melanie, he said, you have reflected; you will tell your secret if the Pope commands you?
Melanie:	I do not know, Sir.
Q.	What! will you disobey the Pope?
Melanie:	The Blessed Virgin has forbidden me to tell it.
Q.	The Blessed Virgin would have us obey the Pope.
Melanie:	It is not the Pope who asks the secret; other persons have told him to ask me for it.

After several other fruitless attempts, Melanie retired in great perplexity of conscience.

On the 26th of March the Abbé Rousselot repaired to the Convent of the Sisters of Providence at Corenc. The Superioress remarked to him, that she knew for what he had come.

"And how do you know?" asked the Abbé.

"Since her interview, with the Abbé Auvergne," replied the Superioress, "Melanie has been in great distress. The companion of her chamber heard her speak in dreams repeatedly:" 'They want my secret . . . I must tell my secret to the Pope, or be severed from the Church!' (This was her own conclusion, for the Abbé Auvergne had said nothing about separation from the Church, or about excommunication.) "More than forty times," continued the Superioress, "she repeated the words — *'to be seperated from the Church'!*

"Are you satisfied with Melanie?" asked the Abbé.

"Yes," replied the Superioress, "we are well satisfied with her; she is the edification of all her companions, and even of the Community. She breathes but for the moment to take the habit. But her intention is to go to a missionary country, that she may consecrate herself to the instruction of little pagan girls."

The Abbé then saw Melanie, and said to her:

"My child, since Sunday, you have doubtless been in trouble; you are uncertain whether, by revealing your secret to the Pope, you will displease the Blessed Virgin, who has forbidden you to tell it. Well, I have come to enlighten you, and to free you from your perplexity. Know, then, my child, that we do not displease the Blessed Virgin, by obeying the Church, to which we must submit all revelations, all apparitions, and all visions. Thus have the saints done. It is Jesus Christ who established the Pope His vicar on earth: the Blessed Virgin knows this well; she is not dissatisfied when we obey him who is the representative of her Son on earth; she will only be so if we disobey him. Thus, then, Melanie, if the Pope asks you for your secret, will you tell it to him?"

Melanie:	Yes, Sir.
Q.	Will you tell him willingly?
Melanie:	Yes, Sir.
Q.	And you will tell it to him without fear of offending the Blessed Virgin?
Melanie:	Yes, Sir.
Q.	If, then, the Pope commands you to tell your secret to any one whom he appoints to receive it, and to convey it to him, will you tell it to that person whom he appoints to come to you for it?

Melanie:	No Sir; I will tell it to the Pope only, and when he commands it.
Q.	And if the Pope gives this command, how will you manage that your secret may reach him?
Melanie:	I will tell it to him myself, or I will write it in a sealed letter.
Q.	And to whom will you give this sealed letter, that it may reach the Pope?
Melanie:	To the Bishop.
Q.	Will you entrust it to no one else?
Melanie:	I will give it to the Bishop or to you.
Q.	Will you not give it to the chaplain of the convent?
Melanie:	No, Sir.
Q.	Will you not let it go to the Pope through the Cardinal Archbishop of Lyons?
Melanie:	No, Sir.
Q.	Nor through any other Bishop or Priest?
Melanie:	No, Sir.
Q.	And why?
Melanie:	Because at Lyons they do not believe much in La Salette, and then I do not want them to unseal my letter.
Q.	But when the Pope knows your secret, will it distress you if he publishes it?
Melanie:	No, Sir, that concerns him, it will be his affair.

Here Melanie bent down her head, and with a smile she asked: *But if this secret regards himself.*

"In this case," replied the Abbé, "the Pope will tell it or not, as he sees fit. Thus, then, my child, you are fully resolved to tell your secret to the Pope?"

Melanie: Yes, Sir, if he commands it; but if he leaves me free, I will not tell it.

The Abbé Rousselot next went to the Petit Séminaire. He asked the superiors if they were satisfied with Maximin. "We are well satisfied with him," replied the Superior, "only he is backward in his class, because he has not studied the rudiments, but he will succeed for he has memory and intelligence." And so as to his conduct? was the next question. "He is light," replied the Superior, "and a little heedless. But I believe he has a good foundation of faith which he shows especially in the church, and when he goes to the sacraments." The Abbé then saw Maximin apart, and found him in the same dispositions which he had manifested to the Abbé Auvergne. In conclusion, he reproached him with the levity of his conduct, and told him, that if went on so, he would give occasion for people to think that he had not really seen the Blessed Virgin, and the fact of La Salette would fall to the ground. Upon which Maximin, understanding the Abbé to allude to certain events which had occurred at Ars, repeated a remark that he had made three weeks before to one of the Canons. "La Salette," "*is now like a flower that in winter they cover with dirt and dung, but which, in the summer, springs up the more beautiful.*"

The tempest which arose against La Salette by reason of the affair at Ars, had the effect of bringing the command which required the children to reveal their secrets to our Holy Father the Pope. And it was through the intermediation of the Cardinal Archbishop of Lyons that this formal demand was first intimated. Seeing that the children were so determined not to deliver their secret *open*, as the Cardinal had intimated a wish they should, and that they were as firmly resolved to give it to no one but the Pope, the Bishop of Grenoble appointed certain witnesses, respectable laymen as well as clergymen, to be present, when Maximin and Melanie wrote each their secrets. They were introduced into the same room, and were seated at separate tables. Maximin put his head into his hands in an attitude of reflection, and then wrote his letter so rapidly that his writing was suspected to be too bad and illegible to go before the Holy Father, and he was requested to write his letter over again and more carefully. So far only is positively known of it, that it is written in seven paragraphs, each of which is numbered, and that it begins with these words: "*Most Holy Father, on the 19th of September, 1846, a Lady appeared to me; they say it is the Blessed Virgin; you will judge whether it was by what follows.*" Whilst writing, Maximin asked how the word *Pontiff* was spelled.

It is said that Melanie betrayed much emotion whilst she wrote her letter, but was in no way embarrassed, and wrote rapidly. She suddenly stopped, and asked the meaning of the word *infallibly.* After it had been explained, she said, "I did not know it." She also asked the orthography and the meaning of the word *Antichrist.* The secret of Melanie is of considerably greater length than that of Maximin. They each sealed their letters themselves in the presence of the witnesses, and they were then sealed with the seal of the Bishop of Grenoble. But soon after, Melanie recollected that she had put two events together without specifying that the one had a separate date from the other, and she hastened to the Episcopal palace to make the correction. She refused, however, to tell any one what that date was, "for", she remarked, "it was part of the secret."

In September of the same year her intimate friend, Mlle. Des Brulais, had the following conversation with Melanie in an interview at Corenc:

Q.	My dear friend, are you tranquil in your mind since you have given up your secret?
Melanie:	Yes, I am very tranquil.

Q.   Do you not regret the giving up of the secret which the Blessed Virgin forbade you to tell?

Melanie: No, I do not regret having told it to the Pope.

Q.   But I shall be asked how you could have revealed your secret to the Pope, after having heretofore said that the Blessed Virgin forbade you to tell it to any person, since the Pope is a person?

Melanie: I did not then know what the Pope was, what rights he had in the Church, and that we are bound to obey him.

Q.   I suppose, my dear Melanie, that the Bishop of Nantes, when he hears of what I shall have to tell him, will ask me if you had seen the Blessed Virgin once more, before you determined to reveal your secret to the Pope. What shall I answer his Lordship?

Here Melanie was silent; she cast down her eyes, and a remarkable smile came over her features. The assistant Superioress, who was present, came to her aid, and said:

Q.   My dear friend, give an answer to Mademoiselle, which she can repeat to the Bishop of Nantes, who perhaps would wish to know the truth. Tell us if the Blessed Virgin appeared to you anew to determine you to reveal your secret?

                  There was the same silence and the same expression of modesty and piety.

Q.   Will you at least tell me, my good Melanie, if you *knew* that you could reveal your secret to the Pope, when you made that revelation?

Melanie: Yes, Madam, *I knew*.

When the present writer, unaware at the time that the question had been put before, asked Melanie if she had ever seen the Blessed Virgin since the Apparition, she answered "*I cannot tell that to you.*" At the same time she very strongly compressed her lips:

Maximin, after giving his secret, felt relieved. "Ah! now," he said, in a tone of self-congratulation, "I am freed from trouble! I have no longer a secret. I am like other people! They need no longer come and ask me anything. They can go and put questions to the Pope; he will tell it if he thinks well." At a later period he was asked how he could have told his secret to the Pope, when he had so often declared that he could tell it to no person. To this he replied: "I did not then know the powers of the Pope, nor that he is *not like another person.* But I now see, that as the Pope asks the question, I ought to tell it."

From the bits of information that have fallen, as well as from observations made on the general conduct of the children with reference to their secrets, it is generally at this day understood that, in the words of M. Gerin, written after he had conveyed those secrets to Rome, Maximin's secret announces mercy and the rehabilitation of things, whilst Melanie's announces great chastisements. This explains much of what is observed in the general bearing of the two young people; Maximin's free and disengaged air, and Melanie's more sad and penitential spirit. When Melanie entered religion, she wished to be called the *Victim of Jesus.* But as it was represented to her that the sacred name of victim belonged to certain Religious of severe enclosed Orders, and could not be given to her, she took the name of *Mary of the Cross.* When she once saw a representation of our Lord's sufferings, it reminded her in a distressing way of her secret.

The Bishop of Grenoble deputed M. Rousselot, one of his Vicars-general, and M. Gerin, the Curé of his Cathedral, to convey the secrets to Rome. Both these ecclesiastics have written letters describing the circumstances of their embassy. When they were presented to

His Holiness, he took the sealed letters from their hands, opened them, and began to read that of Maximin.

"*Here,*" he observed, "*is all the candor and simplicity of a child.*"

Then, that he might read the letters more easily, His Holiness went up to a window and opened the shutter.

"Am I obliged," he remarked, "to keep these things secret?"

"Holy Father," replied M. Gerin, "you can do everything, you have the keys to all things."

As he read the letter of Melanie, his lips became strongly compressed, and his face seemed moved with considerable emotion.

"*These are scourges,*" he said, "*with which France is threatened, but she is not alone culpable, Germany, Italy, all Europe is culpable and merits chastisement. I have less to fear from open impiety, than from indifference and human respect . . . it is not without reason that the Church is called militant, and here,*" pointing to his breast, "*you behold its captain. I must read these letters,*" said His Holiness "*more at leisure.*"

On the following day they had an audience with Cardinal Fornari, at which his Eminence said to the two envoys:

"I am terrified with these prodigies; we have everything that is needed in our religion for the conversion of sinners; and when Heaven employs such means, the evil must be very great."

Cardinal Lambruschini also remarked to them:

"I have long known the fact of La Salette, and, as a bishop, I believe it; and as a bishop I have preached it in my diocese, and I have observed that my diocese produced a great impression. Besides," added his Eminence, "I know the secret of the Children. The Pope has communicated it to me."

On their return His Holiness sent a beautiful present to the Bishop of Grenoble, and his blessing to the two children. And then, intimation was conveyed that the Bishop "*might do as he judged best as to La Salette.*"

After his return from Rome, M. Gerin said to Melanie, "I know not what you have written to the Pope, but he appeared much affected by it"; on which so remarkable a smile arose on her lips, that it struck all who beheld it.

"It scarcely seems to have been *flattering,*" continued M. Gerin.

"Flattering!" she exclaimed.

"Yes, *flattering*; do you know what that word means?" rejoined Mr. Gerin.

"Ah, yes!" she replied, "I know; it means to give pleasure; but it ought to give pleasure to a Pope! *a Pope ought to love to suffer.*"

It is Melanie's impression that, when the Apparition disappeared, the last looks of the Blessed Virgin were mournfully cast towards Rome. (See Appendix - Note E.)

CHAPTER X

CONDUCT OF THE ECCLESIASTICAL AND CIVIL AUTHORITIES

The Bishop of Grenoble was one of the most venerable, prudent, and experienced bishops in all France, and his conduct in the affair of La Salette is eminently marked with carefulness and caution. Public opinion became agitated from the commencement, and a considerable number of the porochial clergy took early occasion to consult their Bishop on the course they ought to pursue. Twelve days after the Apparition took place, his Lordship replied to the enquiries by issuing the following circular to all his clergy. It is dated October 9, 1846.

"Monsieur le Curé,

You are doubtless acquainted with the extraordinary facts which are said to have taken place in the parish of La Salette, near Corps.

"I request you to open the Synodal Statutes which I gave to my Diocese, in the year 1829. You will find the following passage on page 94:

" 'We prohibit, under pain of suspension to be incurred *ipso facto*, any one from declaring a new miracle, or causing to be printed or published any account thereof, under whatsoever pretext of notoriety, except by the authority of the Holy See or of our own, and that, after an exact and rigid examination.'

"Since, then, we have not pronounced on the events in question, both wisdom and duty prescribe to you the greatest reserve, and, above all, an absolute silence in the pulpit with reference to this subject.

"Nevertheless, a lithographic print has been allowed to make its appearance and verses have been added to it.

'I announce to you, Mons. le Curé, that this publication has not only been made without my approval, but that it has exceedingly displeased me, and that I have formally and severely expressed my disapproval. Be, then, upon your guard, and set an example of that prudent reserve which you will not fail to recommend to others.

Receive, Mons. le Curé, the assurance of my sincere and affectionate attachment.

"PHILIBERT, Bishop of Grenoble."

Meanwhile the Bishop carefully collected information on the question of fact. He received numerous letters and circumstantially-detailed reports; he listened to the recitals of pilgrims from his own diocese, as well as from other parts; he caused the places to be visited, and the children to be interrogated, not only by the Curé of Corps and of La Salette, but also by the most respectable clergy of the adjoining districts; he required the most distinguished ecclesiastics of the episcopal city to write out statements of the impressions they had derived from their own investigation. And in the course of three months the illustrious prelate had in hand a voluminous collection of documents on the question of fact.

He then judged it expedient to nominate two commissions, one composed of the Canons of his Cathedral, the other of the Professors of his Episcopal Seminary. He charged them with the duty of examining this collection of documents, and of drawing up a report from them. But each of the commissions was enjoined to give its separate report without any concert with the other.

The Abbé Rousselot has given extracts from these two reports. The opinions and recommendations which they put forth are in their substance identical. They advise the waiting for more decisive evidence — recommend that, in an affair of so grave a nature, nothing should be precipitated — express a conviction that if the work be of God, and have some great providential design in it, He will not fail to clear it up in time — but without deciding either for or against the question of a miraculous manifestation, they gave it as their opinion that as the concourse to the Mountain of La Salette has nothing of evil in it, and is attended with good effects, it should not be interfered with. One of the commissions presented with their reports a series of questions, with the expression of their wish to see them clearly and satisfactorily answered.

From these reports, and the documents they were founded on, M. Rousselot observes that three facts were verified. 1st. That a prompt and extraordinary celebrity had been given to the event of La Salette; that the children had undergone long and numerous interrogatories, ably conducted by persons both capable and wisely distrustful; and that the places which were the reported scenes of the event had been most carefully investigated. 2nd. That a remarkable religious conversion of the inhabitants of the canton of Corps and of the neighboring districts, had followed the event. 3rd. That from the very commencement, reports were generally spread and credited, of extraordinary favors, and even of miraculous healings, obtained by the invocation of our Lady of La Salette, and by the use of the water from the fountain.

Seven months more flowed on, during which the Bishop collected new documents, and interrogated the most grave, competent, and judicious of those who were attracted by its fame to the theater of the event. After having thus waited ten months, the Bishop of Grenoble issued an ordinance appointing M. l'Abbé Rousselot, Professor of Theology, and Honorary Vicar-General, with M. Abbé Orcel, Superior of the Episcopal Seminary, in quality of Commissioners, delegated to make inquiry, and to collect information, relative to the question. They were to associate with themselves those clergymen and laymen whose presence they might judge useful for clearing up the truth. And they were to make inquiries, with the greatest care, of the medical men who had treated the diseases said to have been cured by the invocation of Our Lady of La Salette, and by the use of the water of the fountain. The two commissioners made the tour of nine of the dioceses of the South of France. They next visited the Mountain of La Salette, and examined the two children, and a considerable number of the inhabitants, both of La Salette, and of Corps, and concluded by drawing up their report.

For the examination of this report the Bishop of Grenoble appointed a new commission. It consisted of the two Vicars-General of the diocese, the eight Canons of the Cathedral, the Superior of the Episcopal Seminary, and the Curés of five churches of the city of Grenoble. Several other statements had been prepared and were made use of in addition to the report of the two commissioners. The Bishop presided, and eight conferences were held. They commenced on the 8th of November, 1847, and the discussions were conducted with the greatest caution and solicitude. The children, and those persons who, from their positions, were best informed on the subject, were brought forward, and underwent examination. The principles of evidence were discussed and applied to the case; and as there were some in the assembly who dissented from the general conclusions arrived at, this tended to secure a more searching investigation. The last session, held on the 13th of December, was entirely devoted to the consideration of objections, the solutions of which were adopted by the great majority of the commission. The report, as finally adopted, forms the substance of M. Rousselot's first work, *La Vérité sur L'Evénement de La Salette*. The revolutionary outbreak of February, 1848, induced the author to delay its publication for several months. When at last it appeared, it rapidly obtained a wide circulation, was translated into other languages, and brought conviction to many distinguished persons. It also gave rise to new objections, which served as starting points for further enquiries.

The government had kept a watchful eye upon the affair from an early period. The excitement it had occasioned was too great not to have attracted the attention of Louis Philippe and his ministers. Suspicion arose of some political design, in which La Salette was to figure; and under this suspicion the magistracy of Grenoble were invited by the Procureur du Roi to examine the subject. Accordingly, M. Long the justice of peace at Corps, commenced an investigation, interrogated the children, drew up a report, and in presenting it to the Procureur du Roi, he observed that the accounts given by the children differed in nothing from the satements they had made on the first night after the Apparition. In words they might, but the substance was the same. They repeat the history, he observes, as if they were reciting a lesson; but this, he added is not surprising, for they have recited it so often, and to so many persons, that they have contracted a habit of reciting. In short, nothing could be discovered that furnished any grounds of hope that an imposition might be detected. And hence the Abbé Rousselot significantly remarks that the *authorities have observed silence*. But to this day the government looks upon La Salette, and its influences, with no very favorable eyes, and if they could find a means of detecting the human origin of the Apparition, they are well disposed to do so.

The publication of the report by the Abbé Rousselot forms an important era in the history of La Salette. It drew forth expressions of approval from a considerable number of prelates, to whom the Bishop of Grenoble had sent it. From His Holiness, to whom a copy was presented, it brought a letter to the author, replete with encouragement. "We greatly congratulate you," says the Holy Father, "that in writing your book you have labored to amplify the glory of the Most Blessed Virgin. Delightful to us was all that you relate of the most numerous concourse of people who came thither from all parts to venerate the Most Blessed Virgin; and especially grateful to our soul was it to hear from you, that they there implore the most powerful patronage of the Mother of God for the person of our humility. And we very much desire them to know that we bestow upon them our apostolic benediction.

The report, however, although authenticated and authorized by the episcopal authority, raised up a storm of controversy. Portions of the press fell upon it with avidity, and pamphlets appeared on both sides of the question. But the adverse writers did nothing to overthrow the substantial facts of the case. Not a single name of any weight or authority appeared, or even has appeared, on that side of the controversy. The publications which came forth showed no great signs of piety in their authors, for their tendency was towards rationalism, and if they struck at anything it was at the foundation of all miracles whatsoever; and besides, they abounded in personalities. So far, then, from weakening, they served but to strengthen the cause of the Apparition with men of faith and piety.

This controversy had the effect of bringing out the work, from the pen of M. Rousselot, entitled, "New Documents on the event of La Salette." Authenticated with the authorization of the Bishop, it contained, with other documents, a second list of newly-attested miracles, affirmed to have been wrought through the invocation of our Lady of La Salette, and the use of the water from the fountain. At the commencement of the year the incident of Ars, to which we shall devote a chapter, raised a new commotion. This had the unlooked-for effect of bringing the secret to Rome. On the arrival of the two envoys deputed to carry the secrets to Rome, His Holiness addressed these words to the Abbé Rousselot: "*I have caused the books you have written to be examined by Monsignor Frattini the Promoter of the Faith; they are good, and contain the characters of truth.*" And in an audience which the two envoys afterwards had with the Promoter of the Faith, after Monsignor Frattini had himself repeated to them the report he had delivered, "that the books were clothed with the characters of truth," they asked him if the Bishop of Grenoble could not then build a chapel on the Mountain of La Salette, and publish a

Pastoral on the subject of the apparition? To this the Promoter of the Faith replied:

" I reply in the affirmative to both questions. I see no difficulty in the Bishop of Grenoble going forward and causing a sanctuary of vast and beautiful proportions to be constructed on the place of the Apparition, nor in there being hung up as many ex-votos as there are miracles related in your books, or as may take place hereafter." On another occasion, the same prelate made the following remark: "For forming a new sanctuary in honor of the Blessed Virgin a probability is sufficient; for there is no question of canonizing the Blessed Virgin. But the fact of La Salette re-unites a multitude of probabilities." And again, with reference to the publication of a Pastoral, the Promoter of the Faith remarked: *That the Bishop of Grenoble might do for La Salette what Cardinbal Patrizi had done at Rome, who, as Cardinal Vicar of the Holy City, after assembling a commission, had declared the conversion of M. Ratisbonne to be a miracle which was due to the intercession of the Blessed Virgin. For,"* he added, *"even in the canonization of saints the first procedures are instituted by the ordinary of the place."* In fine, the two envoys returned from Rome to Grenoble the bearers of a verbal intimation from the Holy See to their Bishop, that he *"might do what he judged expedient to La Salette."*

In the September following, a great number of the clergy of the diocese of Grenoble were assembled in the episcopal city for their spiritual exercises, and of these the great majority addressed to the Bishop the following petition:

"Monseigneur,

"The chapter of your Cathedral and the undersigned clergy of your Diocese, present at the retreat, yielding to their conviction and confirmed in their belief by the encouragement which your delegates have received at Rome, beg of you with respectful earnestness that you would publicly announce that you authorize the pilgrimage of La

Salette, that you propose in a short time to build a sanctuary in that place, and that you invite the faithful of your Diocese, of France, and of other countries, to aid you in this great work, by subscription and alms."

To this document 240 of the clergymen present attached their signatures, whilst 17 of them signed a counter petition.

At length, moved by the wishes of the vast majority of his clergy, supported by the unanimous judgment of his Chapter, and after consulting with one of his venerable colleagues in the Episcopacy, who had made the journey to La Salette, the Bishop of Grenoble pronounced his doctrinal judgment.

It was on the fifth anniversary of the Apparition that the celebrated Pastoral Letter was sent forth. It appears to be well attested that, before its publication, it was submitted in private to His Holiness, and received a correction from his pen. It was read in the six hundred churches and chapels of the diocese, and, with some exceptions, spread a universal joy. In that ever memorable document, Monseigneur de Bruillard explains the motives which had guided his conduct from first to last in this important affair; he recapitulates the history of those investigations over which he had watched with so much solicitude; he enumerates the considerations which had moved him at length to take this important step; he remarks that, "docility and submission to the admonitions of Heaven may preserve us from these new chastisements with which we are threatened, whilst too prolonged a resistance may expose us to evils without a remedy." And therefore, "at the express demand," observes this holy prelate, "of all the members of our venerable Chapter, and of the very great majority of the clergy of our Diocese; to satisfy also the just expectation of so great a number of pious souls, both of our own country and of other nations, who might otherwise end in reproving us for having detained the truth in captivity; having invoked anew the Holy Ghost and the assistance of the Blessed Virgin ever Immaculate —

"We declare as follows:

"We judge that the Apparition of the Blessed Virgin to two cowherds, on the 19th of September, 1846, on a mountain of the chain of the Alps, situated in the parish of La Salette, in the arch-presbytery of Corps, bears within itself all the characteristics of truth, and the faithful have grounds for believing it indubitable and certain.

"We believe that this fact acquires a new degree of certitude from the immense and spontaneous concourse of the faithful on the place of the Apparition, as well as from the multitude of prodigies which have been the consequence of the said event, a very great number of which it is impossible to call in doubt without violating the rules of human testimony.

"Wherefore, to testify our lively gratitude to God and to the glorious Virgin Mary, we authorize the *cultus* of our Lady of La Salette. We permit it to be preached, and that practical and moral conclusions may be drawn from this great event.

* * *

"In fine, as the principal end of the Apparition is to recall Christians to the fulfillment of their religious duties, to the frequenting the divine worship, and to the observance of the commands of God and His Church, to a horror of blasphemy, and to the sanctification of the Sunday; we conjure you, our very dear brethren, with a view of your heavenly, and even of your earthly interests, to enter seriously into yourselves, to do penance for your sins, and especially for those against the second and third commandments of God. We conjure you, our well beloved brethren, be docile under the voice of Mary who calls you to penance, and who, on the part of her Son, threatens you with spiritual and temporal evils, if remaining insensible to her maternal admonitions, you harden your hearts, etc., etc.

(Signed)

"PHILIBERT, *Bishop of Grenoble.*"

From the manner in which he had conducted the great affair of La Salette, observes its historian, the Bishop of Grenoble had neither to apprehend the judgment of Rome nor of his venerable colleagues. He sent copies of his Pastoral letter to the Bishops of France, to eminent personages in the Holy City, and to several foreign prelates. And very soon after he received congratulations and adhesions, either public or private, from a great number of Bishops, of Vicars-General, of various Religious orders, both of men and women, and of illustrious personages in the world. The Archbishop of Milan addressed to him a remarkable letter. The Bishop of Ghent reprinted the Pastoral and circulated it amongst his own clergy. The Bishop of Lucon published a Pastoral of his own, in the spirit of that of the Bishop of Grenoble. Other Bishops inserted extracts from it in their own Pastorals. It was published without delay in the Catholic journals of every country in Europe. And in more than one place churches or chapels began to rise in honor of our Lady of La Salette.

Five months after the first Pastoral, the Bishop promulgated a second, on the subject of erecting the Sanctuary on the site of the Apparition, and solicited the Alms of the faithful of his Diocese, as well as of all Christendom, to aid him in this great and noble work.

At length, on the twenty-fifth of May, 1852, the venerable prelate, in company with the Bishop of Valence, ascended to the Holy Mountain, and laid the foundation-stone of the Sanctuary. It was one of those animating and wonderful scenes which are only witnessed at La Salette. The terrace of the Apparition, the ravine of the Sezia, le Planeau, and the base of le Gargas were densely covered with people; the whole ascent, as viewed from the higher points, was alive, like an ant's nest, with the movements of groups and processions winding their way up the valleys. The young women were clothed in white, the greater part of the men in penitential habits. The pastor who headed each procession intoned the Litanies or the Magnificat and the chants resounded for many miles over that wild district. "Seldom," said the Bishop in his Pastoral on the occasion, "ever since the origin of

Christianity, has it occurred that a Bishop has been called upon to proclaim the truth of an Apparition of the august Mother of God. This happiness Heaven has reserved for us, without any merit of our own, as a sensible proof of its mercy towards our beloved diocesans. It is a mission infinitely honorable which it has been given us to fulfill; it is a *duty* which we have to discharge; it is a *right* which is conferred upon us by the holy canons, and which we ought to make use of, lest we culpably resist the will of Heaven, and offer an unjustifiable opposition to the demands which have reached us from every part.

* * *

"But, dearly beloved brethren, however important may be the erection of this *Sanctuary*, there is something more important still; it is the institution of the ministers of religion who are destined to serve it, to receive the pious pilgrims, to speak to them the word of God, to exercise in their favor the minstry of reconciliation, to administer to them the august Sacrament of our altars, and to be towards all *the faithful dispensers of the mysteries of God* and of the spiritual treasures of the Church. These priests will be called the *Missioners of our Lady of La Salette*. Their institution and existence will be like the Sanctuary itself, an eternal monument, a perpetual remembrance of the merciful Apparition of Mary. Selected to be the models and the helpers of the clergy both in town and country, they will have their habitual residence in the episcopal city. They will dwell on the Mountain during the season of the Pilgrimage, and in the winter they will evangelize the different parishes of the Diocese . . . This body of Missioners is as the seal we put to those other works which, by the grace of God, we have been allowed to create. It is the last page of our testament, the legacy we leave to our beloved diocesans. We wish to live again in you by those holy men who, when they speak to you of God will remind you to pray for us."

There are now six Missioners of our Lady of La Salette laboring on the Holy Mountain, and they have fully realized the anticipation of their venerable founder.   (See Appendix - Note F.)

CROWNED VIRGIN OF LA SALETTE

CHAPTER XI

THE CURÉ OF ARS AND LA SALETTE

No objection has been raised against the veracity of the children worth mentioning, except one, and it involves a curious history. The question regards Maximin and his interview with the Curé of Ars. My readers may first wish to know something about this remarkable priest. Ars is a small and very poor village, in the neighborhood of Trévoux on the Saone, and about eighteen miles from Lyons. The Abbé Vianney has been its Curé for the last five and twenty years. Not only has he raised his parish from a state of the greatest laxity and indifference, to habits of fervent piety and devotion; but by the fame of his sanctity, and of his light as a spiritual director, vast numbers of persons are attracted to Ars, and flock to him daily from all parts. Like the children of La Salette, his early years were employed in guarding the beasts of the field. Then he became a conscript for the army, but, horrified with the kind of life he saw around him, young Vianney deserted. A venerable monk of the Chartreuse, observing his piety, became as a father to him. He was released from his engagement to the musket, and after a while obtained an entrance into an ecclesiastical seminary. His abilities were small and his progress slow, and even twice he was sent back for failure in his examinations. But his great piety carried him at last, through all his difficulties, to the priesthood.

On the 18th of May, 1854, I make a visit in company with a friend to this holy priest. Starting from Lyons, all along the road we met with persons returning from a similar visit. Ars is like a place of pilgrimage. From Lyons and all the principal towns in the neighborhood, so great are the numbers of people who visit the Curé, that it has been found necessary to provide daily public vehicles to his church. Conveyances, private as well as public, are frequently met, whilst the poor are seen plodding on foot in the same direction.

We reached Ars a little before eleven, and a good priest, the Curé's assistant, led us by a side door into the church. The first object on which my eyes fell, was the head, face, and shrunken figure of the Curé, straight before me, a figure not easily to be forgotten. He was saying his office, and the nave of the church was crowded and heated with the number of people it contained. His face was small, wasted and sallow; many expressive traces were marked around his mouth. His thin hair was white as snow, his expansive forehead pale, smooth, and clear, whilst his eyes were remarkably deep in shadow and covered with their lids. He soon moved to a little side tribune in the nave, and holding his breviary in his left hand, and leaning, or rather supporting himself erect, against a pillar of the nave, as if to sustain his feeble frame, he began to preach. As he opened his eyes, they sent forth a light, pale indeed, as if from his incessant fasting, but so preternaturally bright and tranquil as to awaken at once the deepest interest. As he went on, the vigor and vivacity of his spirit, mantling through his thin and suffering frame, increased in energy. His voice, soft, shrill, rose into cries of anguish as he spoke of sin, his contracted hand was placed between his eyes, his brows shrank together, and his tears began to fall, as they always do when the thought of sin comes to his mind. He opened again his eyes, and those shaded recesses became full of light; and he threw his feeble hand appealingly towards the people, who, fixed in the positions they had first taken, listened with profound attention, and even awe. Then his eyes were cast up, and his whole figure seemed to follow. He spoke of God, so good so amiable, so loving, and his hands, his shoulders, his very person, seemed to gather on his heart. It was impossible not to feel that God alone was there, and was drawing the whole man to that seat of His repose. Then, there was a word about being in the Heart of Jesus, and in that word one felt that he was *there*. He spoke for twenty minutes, and with a simplicity, a self-abandonment, an energy, and variety of tone and action, as his subject varied, all spontaneous, all from the heart. One thing I cannot describe — such a force of spirit, with such an absence of animal warmth; it was as if an angel spoke through a body wasted even to death. Owing to the loss of his teeth, and to my distance from him, I could not well make out the words of his discourse, but if I had not understood a syllable, I should have known, I should have felt that one was speaking who was living in God. His instruction was on confession, and was interspersed with one or two brief anecdotes and many ejaculations. He then went out, and in his surplice, bareheaded, for he never covers his head, proceeded through the hot sun to visit a sick person. A crowd followed, and pressed upon him.

Before he reached his house, I had looked over it with his Reverend assistant. The walls were naked and ruinous; there was scarcely anything there besides the poor furniture in his own room and his little bed. In one room, however, as ruinous as the rest, there was a good piece of furniture, containing sets of rich vestments, which the Marquis of Ars, at a cost of 40,000 francs, had presented to his church. Before he came in, I was told he would escape from me as soon as he could for a little solitude. But no. His manner of receiving me was as free and simple as it was full of humility and charity. There was nothing of a tone and gesture straining itself to maintain a character, but the disengaged self-abandonment and simple politeness of a saint. The chair which he presented was recommended as the chair of his predecessor in the parish. And often he repeated that he was very grateful for my visit. I was speaking of prayer for England, and of the sufferings of our poorer Catholics on account of their faith; and he was listening, his eyes nearly closed, when suddenly he opened their singular light in all brightness full upon me, and breaking in on the narrative in a way I shall never forget, with the manner of one giving a confidence, he said: "But I believe that the Church in England will return again to its ancient splendor." It is remarkable how often one meets this conviction in France, and how much prayer it gives rise to. To understand him one should see his face, always glowing when he speaks of God, always bursting into fits of tears when he thinks of evil. His poor eyes, though so sweet and tranquil, are worn with his tears and habitually inflamed.

His spirit of direction has that largeness in it which only prayer and a long experience of souls can attain to, unless it be infused. So long as the soul has God for her object, and acts with God, the mode of her interior employment is but an accident. The love of God and the protection of Mary, these two are his two great themes. His own favorite amongst the rest of the Saints is St. Philomene. He has built a beautiful chapel in her honor, attached to his little convent; it is the first that was raised under her invocation in France. Like his church, it breathes of order, cleanliness, and piety. I felt it would be wrong to detain him from his short time for rest and food, so I asked him for a medal by which to remember him. He took a few in his hand, and said:

"Take one."

"No," I said, "give me one."

"There," he said, "is the Immaculate Conception; and there is St. Philomene."

It is not true that this holy priest has predicted evils on France, as has been related; or that he has a special medal, which he blesses for the protection of those who wear it against coming calamities. At my request, he saw my companion for a short time, and saying he would go and meet him, he had no sooner shown himself at the door than the crowd of people rushed upon him. He can never stir out without being thus surrounded and pressed on by the people. He took my friend affectionately by the hand, and walked with him around his little garden, and when an offering was made to him for his church, he said, "Oh, let it be for my poor." He was then left to himself, but his meal was quickly over, and he returned to the confessional. He is now required by his Bishop, under obedience, to add to the one single poor meal that used to be all he had in the day, a second, and to eat a little meat at one of them. At this he sheds tears that a sinner like him should eat meat; and he thinks himself a glutton.

He never begins his labors in the confessional later that two o'clock in the morning, often at one, and when the numbers waiting are very great, at midnight. Penitents will lie all night on the grass, fifty at once, either in order to gain the earliest admission to the church and the confessional, or because of the houses being already completely filled with those who come from a distance. Except while he says Mass, or preaches his little discourse, or for the very short time he takes for his scanty food, the holy Curé lives almost entirely in the confessional. From midnight or early morn he is there until nine at night; then he retires for his office, a little reading, and some two hours at the very most for rest. Such has been the unbroken course of his life for many years. In his soul he lives with God; his poor earthly frame suffers from a complication of most acute maladies, which give him no repose. As he said to one who is intimate with him, he suffers all day for the conversion of souls, and all night for the souls in purgatory. Of his penetration into the interior states of souls many instances are recounted.

Some five years ago, the holy Curé, to the surprise of all who saw the action, put on his hat, took his breviary under his arm, and started off. His Vicaire, suspecting his object, followed him; his aged housekeeper soon followed also. The priest got before him, and accosted him:

"Where, my father, are you going?"

"I have long taken care of others," he replied; "I must look to my own soul."

"But have you the Bishop's permission to go?" said his Reverend companion.

"You," he replied, "know the people of this parish well; you are competent to take care of them."

He was bent on seeking solitude in the Chartreuse. His housekeeper seized possession of his breviary.

"Give it up," said the holy Curé, "I command you."

"Father, I never disobeyed you until now," replied his house-keeper.

Then the Vicaire got on the narrow bridge on his path to stop the way, and meanwhile the church bell was rung, and the parish alarmed; the people crowded to the place of this singular contest with tears and entreaties. At last the Vicaire said:

"If you go I will not remain; I will go too; and what will become of your people?"

Then said the holy Curé, with a burst of tears, "I cannot leave my people abandoned," and with that he returned.

The Sanctuary of his church is most clean and orderly; a new marble altar is adorned with sculptures of his patron saints; a new stained window decorates the apse; the chapels are full of pious objects. In one is all that can recall the sufferings of our Lord; in another that of our Lady of Dolors and of St. Philomene, there is hung up a little forest of crutches, generally offerings from those who required them on their way to Ars, but not on their return homewards. On one column hangs a tabular inscription, in which the holy Curé dedicates himself and his parishioners to our Lady of the Immaculate Conception. Whilst on the other side, by the statue of our Lady of Dolors, there is a painting, more expressive than skillfully executed, which represents the Curé in bed, in the last extremity, and receiving the Holy Viaticum; priests, Religious sisters, and his parishioners on their knees look mournfully on with prayer on their lips, whilst above this scene appears our Lady in an attitude of protection. The inscription intimates that this is the grateful expression of his parishioners to our Lady Conceived without stain, for his instantaneous recovery on the 9th of May 1843.

There came a report that Maximin has retracted his statement respecting the Apparition, in the presence of this venerable Curé. This report got widely spread, and was much harped upon by the opponents of La Salette. The story arose out of the following incident.

Certain enthusiasts for the Baron of Richemont, the pretended Louis XVII, got it into their heads that the secret of La Salette concerned their idol. Three of these gentlemen contrived to draw Maximin to Lyons; there they surrounded him with their own friends, tried their mesmeric arts upon him, and did all in their power to elicit his secret, and connect it with their own cause. At length he was accidentally met and rescued from their hands by his early friend the Abbé Bez, the author of one of the earliest books in favor of La Salette. While he was with them, under the pretence of enabling him to obtain some light on his vocation, they conducted Maximin to the Curé of Ars. As the Abbé Rousselot observes, he went in a thoughtless humor, and he came back in a humor just as thoughtless. But, neither while going nor returning did he evince that contrition and repentance for deceptions practised which have been ascribed to him, and one of the three persons who conducted him thither has since declared that when he left Ars he was both joyous and contented, and gave no cause for suspicion that he had been making any painful or humiliating avowal. Maximin shall now tell his own story. He is met, some time after the event we have narrated, at the Grande Chartreuse, by his long-tried friend Mlle. Des Brulais. She interrogates him as follows:

Q.   Why did you give yourself into the hands of those persons?

Maximin: Why, indeed, I wished to see the country.

Q.   Into what strange ways you threw yourself, poor impudent youth that you are! What were you thinking of?

Maximin: Ah, I committed a foolery, that's true; but all the same, it was that which brought the secret to Rome

Q.   How so?

Maximin: Well, then, you will see; Monseigneur the Cardi-
                nal (of Lyons) heard of all the noise in the news-
                papers, because of the Curé of Ars, and he wished
                to have the secret. The Pope demanded it, and the
                Bishop of Grenoble sent it to the Pope; that is what
                I mean.

Q.   But what happened with the Curé of Ars? Will you
                tell me something about it?

Maximin: This is what happened. These three gentlemen
                took me to the Curé of Ars, that I might consult
                him, as they said, upon my vocation. The Curé
                advised me to return to my diocese; and the
                gentlemen were quite angry; they told me I had
                not understood him, and bid me go back again to
                him. I went to his confessional, for he is seldom
                seen by persons except there. The Curé of Ars is
                almost deaf, and people don't understand him
                very well, because he has lost most of his teeth. He
                asked me if I had seen the Blessed Virgin, and I
                answered him: "I do not know whether it was the
                Blessed Virgin; I saw something . . . a Lady. But
                if you know yourself that it was the Blessed
                Virgin, you should tell it to all the people, that they
                may believe in La Salette."

Q.   But it is said as a certainty, my dear child, that you
                accused yourself to the Curé of Ars of having told
                lies; is that true?

Maximin: Ah! I said to the Curé that I had sometimes told
                lies. '*You must retract*,' said he. 'But no,' I an-
                swered, 'I cannot retract for that; it is not worth the

trouble.' He told me I *ought*, and I answered him: 'Since it is past, I cannot do it now; it is too old .'

Q.   But what did you mean?

Maximin answered with a tone of assurance, "I meant my little stories to the Curé of Corps, when I did not want to say where I was going, or when I did not want to study my lessons."

Q.   Thus, I see, the Curé of Ars understood those stories of which you spoke, as referring to the Apparition?

Maximin: Why, yes! he understood it in that way, as that was put in the newspapers.

Q.   But you were not at confession?

Maximin: No, I was at the confessional, but I had not said my *Confiteor*, and I did not go there to make my confession.

Q.   They add a story that you retracted before the Vicaire of Ars?

Maximin: Ah! he said that I had made out a story, and that I had not seen the Blessed Virgin; and then, as I was not in a very good humor, I said to him: "*Have it if you will, that I don't tell the truth, and that I did not see anything,*" and then I went away.

This was Maximin's well-known style of answering whensoever his veracity was called in question, and there are many examples of it reported in his examinations. The cause of his giving way to those tart replies on occasion, Maximin has himself explained more than once to his friends. He finds that when the Apparition and his own truthfulness are called in question in an offensive manner, that a certain dread comes upon him, lest in his inward excitement and confusion he should be thrown off his guard, and should let some portion of his secret slip from him; and so he saves himself by cutting off the interrogator with some short and abrupt reply, which puts an end to his trial. And it must be recollected that, in the present instance, he was in a very peculiar position, was in a strange place, and must have felt his loneliness, surrounded as he was by designing men, who were utter strangers to him, and knew nothing of his character. But before we proceed, we will give in his own words the history of his escape from the gentlemen who had thus far got him into their hands. He is still replying to the questions of the same friend:

"I returned to Lyons with these gentlemen, and they took me to dinner at hotel du Parc. They sat down at table, and could not agree, because all three *wanted to have me*. When all of a sudden, look you, the waiter opened the door of the room, and I saw M. Bez come in, the priest who has come several times to La Salette, and whom I am very fond of. As soon as I saw M. Bez I ran crying into his arms; and when he saw me he was quite moved. And then I would not leave him again, and all the three stood pretty well astonished. Then the Bishop of Grenoble had me placed in the Petit Seminaire; and I wrote a letter to the Curé of Ars, to assure him that I had never retracted, because it is true."

Q.   How did M. Bez happen to be at that hotel at the same time with you?

Maximin: I don't know; it was the good God who did that. I believe he went to hire an apartment for a friend; and certainly he could not have known that these gentlemen had just brought me to that hotel, or even that I was in Lyons.

Maximin remained three weeks under the care of a clergyman at a pension at Lyons, and then returned to Grenoble. Here he underwent a severe examination in presence of the Bishop before a commission of clergy and laity. He was tried and urged in every way to induce him to avow the retraction which, it began to be rumored, he had made. But Maximin remained firm and intrepid. He protested that he would never avow but what he had always avowed, and what he would avow on his deathbed, that he had seen a *beautiful Lady*, who spoke and disappeared. He maintained that he had given no contradiction to this at Ars, but admitted that, not understanding the Curé distinctly, he had repeatedly said yes and no at hazard. He afterwards underwent other and repeated interrogations at the episcopal palace, but without any other result. Maximin was merely found to be what he had always been.

After this, Maximin, unknown to any one, wrote a letter to one of those gentlemen who had conducted him to Lyons, and who had been kind to him. It is in his off-hand style interspersed with errors of diction, but evidently from his heart. In it he says:

March 13, 1851

"My Dear sir,

"They have told you that I belied myself before the Curé of Ars. I think myself all this comes from the Vicaire for you know what he said to us at the Providence (The convent where the Vicar, the assistant of the Cure, resides), where he took us. But as for me, I assure you that I in no way belied myself, and I am always ready to give my blood to maintain what I saw. For the Curé of Ars may have ill-understood me, or the devil may have changed my words in his ears. But as for me, I assure you that I did not unsay what I have said for the last four years that I had seen. Remember, Sir, that the money which has been offered us to say that what we had seen was not, we might have had it, poor as we are, and you know our families. I beg of you to judge all this, and you will see that what we have said for four years is the same truth," etc., etc.

These statements of Maximin bring out his character with considerable force, whilst they explain the cause of the misunderstanding at Ars.. But the good Curé of Ars, it is alleged, wrote a letter to the Cardinal Archbishop of Lyons, expressing his disbelief, of the fact of La Salette; and this point remains to be enquired into.

Not more than a month after Maximin had been with the good Curé, a respectable person from Lyons had an interview with the latter, and the following record of the conversation was transmitted to the Abbé Rousselot.

Q.	Do you believe in La Salette?
The Curé:	Yes; I believe in it.
Q.	And yet the Cardinal has received a letter signed by you, and in that letter you say it is not to be believed, because it is false.
The Curé:	*Every day I sign a quantity of letters, though I do not read any of them; but I believe in La Salette.*

The fact is, that this holy Curé never himself writes anything, as I was informed by his present Vicaire; he does not answer any of the numerous letters which are addressed to him; and it appears that the Vicaire to whom Maximin refers in his letter, and who was well known to be an opponent of La Salette, after his interview with Maximin, drew up a letter of his own to the Cardinal Archbishop, and got the simple hearted Curé to put his name to that letter, though he had never read it. That Vicaire was afterwards removed, and another put in his place.

Immediately after this affair took place, one of the Marist Fathers went expressly to Ars to enquire into its truth, and the Curé expressed himself to him in these words: "*I have always believed in La Salette; I believe in it still.* I bless medals and images of our Lady of La Salette; I have distributed a great number of them. I have written all this to the Bishop of Grenoble. *And see here whether I do not believe!*" Here the Curé approaches his bed, and drawing the curtain, showed the Religious father a large picture of our Lady of La Salette, framed, and hung up at the head of his bed: "I did not insist further," writes this respected Religious to the Bishop of Grenoble, "for I was convinced that the good Curé had scarcely had anything to do with all that I had heard reported of him. I have repeated this to a great number of persons, who all conclude with me that the imagination of certain enemies of La Salette had furnished those darkenings of suspicion which had given so much scandal to pious souls."

But the good Curé was quite disconsolate at all that was attributed to him. He gave expression to his feelings to several persons, of whom one wrote on the 20th of October, 1851, to the Abbé Rousselot as follows: "I have seen the Curé, who is truly disconsolate at what is attributed to him. He told me, as well as Madame D..., that *he had never said* that the event of La Salette had not taken place; only that it was possible that *the child had not well explained himself*, or that *he himself had not well understood him*; that besides, he had never seen Melanie, who would perhaps have been clearer in her answers. Madame.... repeated the very same words to me five days ago."

I will add but one quotation more; it is decisive of the affair at Ars. The Bishop of Grenoble, after sending two of his clergy to make enquiries on the spot, wrote to the Bishop of Belley, in whose diocese the parish of Ars is situated. The following is an extract from the reply of the Bishop of Belley, a prelate bearing a high character for wisdom and sanctity.

Belley, January 15, 1851.

"Monseigneur......

"Before answering the letter you did me the honor to address to me, I wished to make enquiries to what had passed at Ars. I had a somewhat lengthy interview with M. Raymond, who acts as Vicaire, and who interrogated the young man on the subject of La Salette. The Bishops of Valence and of Viviers were with me for the consecration of Monseigneur Challandon; I communicated to them the documents which you sent me, and this is the result of our reflections. 1. We ever consider it as certain that the children are not in any understanding with each other to deceive the public, and that they really saw a person who spoke to them. 2. Was it the Blessed Virgin? Everything leads to that belief; but all this cannot be attested except by miracles different from the Apparition. . . . It is for you, Monseigneur, to examine and pronounce, etc., etc."

A few days after what had passed at Ars, the Bishop of Belley had remarked to a Marist Father: — "What has passed at Ars is but a trial and a tempest raised by the devil; the fact of La Salette will come out of it more brilliant." And two months before his death, the same distinguished Prelate repeated an expression he had often used before: — "I attach no importance to what passed at Ars; the Curé of Ars is not competent to judge a fact of so much gravity."

If I have dwelt at some length on the incident of Ars, it is because it is the sole objection that has been raised against the evidence, and which, in the exaggerated form it gained through rumor, caused doubts to some believers for a time, whilst it deterred others from enquiry. But, as the Bishop of Belley had anticipated, "the fact of La Salette came out of it more brilliant." It was this circumstance that occasioned the demand for the secret to be sent to Rome. And it was the encouragement that came from Rome after the arrival of the secret, which prompted the Bishop of Grenoble in issuing his judicial decision, and founding the Sanctuary. The words of Maximin first uttered after his return from Ars to Grenoble were like a prophecy:

"They now," he said, "mock at La Salette; but it is like a flower which in winter they cover with dirt and dung, but in the summer it springs from the earth more beautiful."

At a later period, Maximin said, in reply to a friendly question:

"The affair goes prosperously! You see what a noise they have made. Oh Well! It is that which has pushed the secret to Rome; without that noise, it would not have been there *yet.*" (While this chapter was going through the press, I received a letter from the Curé of Ars. It is written by the hand of another person, but it is signed by the holy Curé, and bears the date July 10th, 1854. In it he says :— "On the Apparition of the Blessed Virgin at La Salette, since his Lordship, the Bishop of Grenoble preaches it, and the Sovereign Pontiff, it is said, approves of it, I believe that you may speak of it in all surety of conscience.")

CHAPTER XII

ROME AND LA SALETTE

The Holy See has not finally pronounced upon the fact of La Salette. Her word, that final and decisive word, has not been uttered. Yet the countenance and encouragement which the Sovereign Pontiff has given to the devotion of Our Lady of La Salette, is one of the most remarkable features of its history. We have seen how expressions given in private at Rome brought the Bishop of Grenoble to his final determination of issuing his celebrated Pastoral Letter; we have seen how that Pastoral Letter was looked over at Rome before its publication, and we have seen in what spirit the authentic reports of the history of the Apparition, and of the fruits of that devotion to our Lady of La Salette were received and commended in that holy city. And no sooner had the judicial decision of the Bishop of Grenoble been received, than it was published in the religious journals of Rome, without any correction from the rigorous censorship to which it had been submitted. Collections for the new sanctuary were organized in that city, and the same journals announced them to the faithful even with a degree of enthusiasm. But the strongest proof of the countenance given to the new pilgrimage by the Holy See, is the number and extent of spiritual favors which the Sovereign Pontiff has accorded to the Sanctuary of La Salette.

I.   By a Rescript of the 24th August, 1852, the Sovereign Pontiff declared the High Altar of the Sanctuary of La Salette, a privileged Altar in perpetuity.

II.   By a Rescript of 26th August, 1852, he grants permission to say a Votive Mass of the Blessed Virgin, to all priests who come to La Salette, on any day of the year except on the great Festivals and the privileged Ferias.

III. By a Brief of 26th August, 1852, the Sovereign Pontiff grants to the members of the Confraternity of La Salétte:

   1st. A plenary indulgence at the hour of entering the Confraternity;

   2nd. A plenary indulgence at the hour of death;

   3rd. A plenary indulgence once a year, the day of the principal festival of the Confraternity;

   4th. An indulgence of seven years and seven quarantines, four times a year, on four determined days;

   5th. Sixty days of indulgence for every work of piety or of charity accomplished by them.

IV. By the Brief of 3rd September, 1852, His Holiness grants a plenary indulgence once a year to every one who shall visit the church of La Salette.

V. Another Brief of the same date grants:

   1st. A plenary indulgence to the faithful who follow the exercises of the missions or of the retreats, preached by the Missioners of La Salette, provided they have assisted at three, at least, of the sermons;

   2nd. Two hunndred days each time they assist at one of the sermons.

VI. A Brief of 7th September, 1852, erects the Confraternity of La Salette into an Archconfraternity, under the name of our Lady of *Reconciliation* of La Salette.

VII. In fine, by an Indult of 2nd December, His Holiness Pius IX grants, at the request of the Bishop of Grenoble, the permission to solemnize each year, on the 19th of September, the Anniversary of the Apparition (VEL IPSO APPARITIONIS DIE) in all the churches of the diocese; or, to celebrate it on the following Sunday, by a solemn Mass, and by singing the Vespers of the Blessed Virgin. In the same Indult His Holiness authorizes the clergy, if they prefer it, to celebrate the memory of the Apparition (MEMORIUM HUJUS APPARITIONIS RECOLERE) by adopting the entire office, and celebrating the Mass of the *Patronage of the Blessed Virgin*, under solemn rite, as a *Double of the Second Class.*

The reader will not fail to remark how much is implied in the last privilege. The clergy of the Diocese of Grenoble are not indeed enjoined, but they are permitted to celebrate *the Anniversary of the Apparition*, with High Mass, solemn Vespers, the Office, and all the solemnities of a festival of the Blessed Virgin. The law of prayer, according to the great maxim of St. Augustine, is the law of belief. And the Holy See, by permitting the festival to be observed in the Diocese of Grenoble has permitted the belief of the Apparition. (See Appendix - Note G.)

CHAPTER XIII

THE MIRACLES OF LA SALETTE

The greatest miracle which flowed from La Salette is the miracle of grace. By all accounts nothing could be more desolate for a Catholic country than the state of religion in the districts all around La Salette at the time of the Apparition. "Women advanced in age alone attended Mass." The declaration of the Blessed Virgin was admitted to be a fact, and was never contradicted. As a general affirmation it was but too true. Yet a short time after the Apparition took place, and in consequence of it, the religious condition of the whole of that part of the country became entirely changed. The churches were filled with people; the Sacraments were well attended; and swearing was put an end to. If one heard another swear, he would rebuke him, and say:

"Unhappy man! Did not the Blessed Virgin forbid it? Would you bring the famine back again?"

And the other would answer: "I beg pardon, I forgot myself."

Hundreds of thousands of persons have been attracted to the Mountain of La Salette as pilgrims. Let the reader reflect and consider well within himself what state of mind and what disposition of heart, this attraction supposes and implies. There was nothing for earthly gratification, nothing to feed human curiosity on the Mountain. Quite the contrary. Everyone who goes there must give up for the time the most ordinary conveniences of life. The worldly spirit has never found its way there as yet. A strong religious feeling is manifested in all who ascend the Holy Mountain. And it is the impression of those who observe this pilgrimage in its daily progress, that no one goes back without carrying away a certain increase of peace and a certain religious content.

These, at all events, are facts no Catholic will think of attempting to explain by mere natural causes. They of necessity presuppose the intervention of the Divine Grace. Nor will ordinary graces explain a course of conversion so extensive and so thorough as that of which the pilgrimage and the devotion to our Lady of La Salette have been the instruments. The finger of God is here, and the Divine fruits, of which so great an abundance is visible, prove that a Divine seed has been abundantly sown upon that Holy Mountain. Indeed, the conversions from a life of sin or of indifference to a life of piety, which that pilgrimage has witnessed, is one of the greatest religious marvels of our time. Many hardened sinners have also been converted by the prayers, the novenas, and the pilgrimages, which their friends have made to our Lady of La Salette on their behalf. Numbers of these cases are known through private circles, but it has been well observed, that they are of too delicate a nature for public authentication, nor are they susceptible of the same kind of proof which attends a miracle in the order of nature. I shall not, therefore, dwell longer on this part of the subject.

But undoubtedly there have been wrought a considerable number of miraculous healings, either on the Mountain, or in other places, through the invocation of our Lady of La Salette, and by the use of the water of the fountain. And the three books of the Abbé Rousselot are a good deal taken up with narratives of these cures, and with the documents drawn up and attested for proof of them. These proofs are not in all the cases of equal weight, nor are all the cures spoken of alike in their importance and gravity; yet there are proofs, abundant and beyond all that any one can fairly require, to demonstrate, that miraculous cures wrought in direct relation with the Apparition of La Salette have been numerous and striking.

And here let me foretell a remark. All are not cured who go to the Holy Mountain with the desire of obtaining their restoration to health, or who invoke their cure from a distance, even with a strong faith. No. Miraculous intervention works by no such universal rule. This would be to change an exceptional order of things into a law. Men would quickly proclaim it to be some occult power of nature, and not a direct intervention of the Divine will. God has never at any time constituted an ordinance which, like a sacrament, should, on certain conditions, invariably cure the diseases which flesh is heir to. When the angel descended into the Probatica, and stirred its waters, the first who descended was cured, and thus the chain of miracles was kept up to the time of Christ in the Jewish Church. But it was only one who was healed, and only at the time when the angel came and stirred the waters. It is neither in the order of God, nor in the order of salvation, that there should be certain means, even with the exercises of faith and devotion, to obtain a miraculous healing of our corporal miseries. Those miseries are often the greatest blessings in disguise, and the occasion both of salvation and of sanctification to the souls who are tried and purified through their instrumentality.

But a sufficient number of persons, and more than sufficient, are healed, to give an authentication to the Apparition, of a kind totally distinct from the testimony of the children. These miracles witness from heaven, whilst the children witness on earth. But this is a fact of La Salette which ought not to be passed over in the faithful testimony of a pilgrim. Those who go there in quest of healing, though they find it not, return to their homes consoled and satisfied with their lot. I met several who had been healed, and some who sought their cure and did not obtain it; but I did not find one in all that number in whom the piety exercised in that hallowed Sanctuary had not infused a certain holy cheerfulness and content.

In fact, when we look over the list of miracles which has been published, it at once becomes remarkable how evidently they are designed as testimonies. They are found in this place or that, all over France. Forty-six cures are recorded up to September, 1852, and they are distributed over twenty-six dioceses. Nor is the diocese of Grenoble that on whose subjects the greatest number of cures have been wrought. The dioceses of Arras, Digne, and Langres have had more than any others, that is to say, four in each.

With relation to dioceses the cures stand as follows: Marseilles, 1; Perpignan, 1; Fréjus, 3; Avignon, 3; Digne, 4; Grenoble, 3; Lyons, 1; Valence, 1; Viviers, 1; Bordeaux, 1; Bourg, 1; Verdun, 1; Rennes, 1; Sens, 2; Troyes, 2; Langres, 4; Blois, 1; Quimper, 2; Soissons, 1; Orléans, 1; Paris, 2; Amiens, 1; Arras, 4; Cambrai, 2; Namur in Belgium, 1; Lausanne in Switzerland, 1. It will thus be seen, by glancing over the map of France, how these miraculous powers have been exercised in favor of persons, not more of the neighborhood of the Apparition, than of any other portion of France; and it will at the same time become evident how widely extended is this devotion of our Lady of La Salette.

I will now select a few examples of these miracles, and will give a brief account of them. Those who wish to read the attestations may refer to them as they are recorded in the works I have so often quoted.

Sister St. Charles Pierron, of the Hospitaliérs of St. Joseph of Avignon, was reduced to the last stage of decline; for eight years she had been compelled to lie in bed, and besides the severe condition of her lungs, had violent pains of stomach, frequent spittings of blood, dysentary, and a continuous slow fever.

In December, 1846, her sufferings became much aggravated, her throat, tongue, and palate grew ulcerated, and emitted a fetid odor; she had great difficulty in swallowing, as well as in speaking so as to make herself understood; and, from that time until the 16th of April, 1847, the day of her cure, she took no solid food, and only a small quantity of fluid daily. In the month of February, her two physicians, to quote the attestation of one of them, "gave her up to her sad destiny." The Superioress of the community had a great desire to obtain a confirmation of the evidence of the two children of La Salette; and as the maladies of Sister St. Charles had been long and publicly known, she selected her case in preference to that of any other of the sick of her community. But when it was proposed to Sister St. Charles, that her cure should be sought through our Lady of La Salette, this good Religious declared that she had no desire to recover her health, as it would keep her from eternity. The Superioress urged the proposal upon her repeatedly, but as the sister continued to be reluctant, the Superioress used her authority, and told her that she had no right to consider herself, but only the glory of God and the augmentation of the honor of the Blessed Virgin. Sister St. Charles then consented, and expressed a conviction that she should be healed, and a small quantity of the water of La Salette was provided for her to drink. She was requested to point out herself the exercises to be followed during the novena. Each day of that novena, a sister of the community went to holy communion in reparation for the sins of blasphemy and the profanation of the Sunday, which the Blessed Virgin had pointed out. There were three fasts for the same intention, and each day the community recited the *Salve Regina*, three *Aves*, with the invocation, *O Mary conceived without sin*, etc., and the *Mater Admirabilis*.

On the seventh day of the novena, Sister St. Charles was not only worse but swooned and cast a great quantity of blood. Seeing her condition, the Superioress said to her: "I think the Blessed Virgin is going to cure you by sending you to heaven." Whereupon the sister replied: "All my maladies do not weaken my confidence: as I have only three days more to suffer, I pray our good Mother not to spare me." In fact, she would have everything made ready, and begged that her habit and veil, which had not been used for a long time, might be put by her bedside. On the Friday morning, the day before the conclusion of the novena, after a very bad night, she spat blood as usual. The community on that morning anticipated their general communion for her, as the Bishop of Chalons said the Mass in their chapel. This was a trial to Sister St. Charles, as she had hoped the following day to make her communion with them. She was planning in her mind to ask for a general communion again for the following morning, in which she hoped to be able to join, and was full of this thought, when she suddenly felt a great revolution in her frame, her maladies ceased at once, and she felt, to use her own expression, as if an invisible hand had raised her up. She cried out, "I am healed." Sister St. Joseph, who was in bed in the same room, did not understand what she said, and thought, on the contrary, that she was becoming worse; she was the more alarmed, as she was alone at this moment, and too ill herself to go and help her. Sister St. Charles hearing her weep, quitted her own bed and went herself to console her. She did the same to the portress, who looked after the convent during Mass, and was terribly frightened at hearing someone running about the room in which she had only left sick people in bed. She came running in quite out of breath and feeling quite ill. Sister St. Charles calmed her, gave her something to drink, as well as to Sister St. Joseph, and assured them that she was cured. She then went down to the chapel, and heard the remainder of the Mass, kneeling without any support. Her two physicians were astounded when they saw her, and declared in their testimonies that they could not believe their own eyes. She joined the labors of the community, was as active as any other sister, could carry heavy loads, and remained in perfect health.

The cure is declared by the physician-in-chief of the hospital of Avignon, to have taken place in a manner beyond the intervention of art and to partake of the nature of a prodigy. It is certified in similar terms by two other medical men, also by the three Capitular vicars-general, by one of the first barristers of Avignon, and by the Superioress and officials of the community.

The next case I shall cite occurred at Avallon, in the archdiocese of Sens. Antoinette Bollenat, aged thirty-three, had good health until the age of twelve years, when she was thrown down and cruelly beaten by a woman, who pressed her knee violently upon her chest and stomach. After that time Antoinette constantly suffered the most dreadful pains; for seventeen years she vomited whatever she took, and was only able to digest a small quantity of milk or beaf tea. For seven years she had an enormous tumor over her stomach, on one side, which was acutely painful, and continued to increase, despite all the aid of medicine. For three years she had lain on her back without being able to move any of her limbs, except her lower extremities slightly, and she was almost entirely deprived of sleep. After her greatest agonies of pain she was relieved by a swoon. On the 19th of November, 1847, she exhibited all the signs of approaching death. But, some time before, she had proposed a novena to our Lady of La Salette. The Archpriest procured some of the water from the fountain, and during the novena she took a spoonful of it each day. But instead of amending, her state grew worse until the 21st of November, the feast of our Lady's Presentation, and the last day of the novena; when, at half-past four in the evening, she suddenly felt her pains gone, her tumor had disappeared, and she arose quite in good health. After making her thanksgiving, she joined the family table and ate a good meal, and has continued without any return of her ailments. This miracle was the subject of much and careful investigation. I will adjoin the judicial sentence of the Archbishop of Sens.

"Mellon Jolly," by the divine mercy and the favor of the Holy Apostolic See, Archbishop of Sens, Bishop of Auxerre, Primate of the Gauls and of Germany.

"Having regard to the report of the commission appointed by us, the 24th of February, 1848, to conduct a judicial inquiry into the facts relative to an extraordinary cure which took place at Avallon on the 21st of November, 1847, on the person of Antoinette Bollenat, after a novena to the Most Blessed Virgin; likewise to the interrogatories of the witnesses and the physician, dated the 7th, 8th, and 14th of February, 1848; likewise, to the certificates and documents annexed to the interrogatories; likewise, to the report presented to us on the 20th of February, 1849, by the Abbé Chanveau, our vicar-general, charged with the examination of this affair, and the discussion of the facts; likewise to the conclusions drawn in the report; after having taken the advice of our council, and invoked the holy name of God.

"We declare, for the glory of God, the glory of the Most Blessed Virgin, and the edification of the faithful, that the cure of Antoinette Bollenat, wrought the 21st November, 1847, after a novena to the most Blessed Virgin, Mother of God, invoked under the name of Our Lady of La Salette, presents all the conditions and all the characters of a miraculous cure, and constitutes a miracle of the third order.

"Given at Sens, under our seal, and the counter sign of our Vicar-general, the 4th of March, in the year of grace, 1849.

MELLON
Archbishop of Sens

M. Martin, a cleric in minor orders, after long, complicated, and painful sickness, was attacked with a sciatica, which contracted his leg. This additional malady became so serious, and was accompanied with pains so excessive, and so far beyond the power of his weak and nervous state to bear, that his physician had repeatedly declared, that unless the pains could be diminished, they would take him off. A novena to our Lady of La Salette was commenced, and on the first day of the novena, at seven in the evening, the sufferer received some water from the fountain of La Salette, drank it, and was immediately restored to perfect health. This is attested by the Superiors and Professors of the Seminary, and is authenticated in a formal letter of the Bishop of Verdun, who declares his conviction that "it is very difficult to explain such a cure by the sole force of nature."

I shall next select a cure through a pilgrimage to La Salette. Mlle. Lauzer, of St. Ceré, aged 18, was placed at the pension of the Convent of the Visitation at Valence. From her childhood to her 13th year her eyes were affected from ophthalmia. This disorder then disappeared, but from their defectiveness and weakness, she still required the use of a pair of spectacles. On the 17th of April, 1852, this young lady lost the entire use, first of one eye, then of the other, on the same day, and was reduced to such a total blindness, that she became insensible to the light even of the sun. Her physician pronounced it to be a case of *amaurosis*, and that both her eyes were completely paralyzed. After every remedy which the science of medicine could apply had been tried, without the least effect, she herself proposed a pilgrimage to La Salette. The young lady resolved in her piety to walk the whole way from Valence, and she set out in company with, and under the guidance of Sister Mary Justine, a member of the community. She travelled on foot the whole way, employing her heart in prayer; and from Corps, on the morning of the first of July, she made the entire ascent of the mountain, still on foot. She reached the Sanctuary wet to the skin from the heavy rain, and covered with perspiration. She hoped to obtain her restoration on the following day, which was the feast of the Visitation of our Lady. She at once hastened to the chapel, and as she entered she exclaimed, "*How good it is to be here!*" A quarter of an hour afterwards Father Sibillat, one of the missioners, gave her the holy communion, on receiving which her sight instantaneously returned. After a few minutes of emotion, in which she remained transfixed in her position, she exclaimed: "*I see! I see!*" After which she remained intensely absorbed in contemplation. Meanwhile Mass was said, and after it was finished, it required the authority of Father Sibillat, joined to the entreaties of Sr. Mary Justine, to induce her to return from her absorbed devotion, and to show the pilgrims who filled the chapel what God had done for her through the intercession of Mary. Her sight not only remained good, but she very soon found that her spectacles had become an embarrassment rather than a service, and she ceased to use them.

This cure is attested by the physician of Mlle. Lauzer, who calls it miraculous, by fifty-five witnesses, and also by the community at

returned in the night. The least movement gave her torture, the beating of the heart alone caused insufferable anguish. She could not swallow a drop of water, or even her own saliva, and was in constant expectation of her last moment. On the 26th of March, at half-past six in the evening, Sister Mary Francis of Sales had an attack, which, to all appearance, would have been her last. It was the sixth day of the novena. She was delirious; her eyes were fixed, and she had all the symptoms of approaching death. She received Extreme Unction and the indulgence at the hour of death. The sisters withdrew, and prepared everything for the funeral, whilst the Superioress, with four of the community, watched by her. At midnight she was covered with the death-sweat. They saw her face become stiffened. The Mother Superioress put a light to the eyes of her dying Religious, but she could not see it, her eyes were glazed and fixed. They lit the blessed candle, and began the prayers for the agonizing. After a few minutes respiration returned; she fell into a kind of doze; the pulse grew intermittent; sometimes it was several minutes without beating; and then beat rapidly. The physician entered; she did not know him, for her eyes were glazed and her delirium continued. He said she could not possibly get over the day. During the twenty hours of her agony she could not swallow a drop of water; everything flowed back from her mouth; all they did was to apply the water of La Salette to her lips. Yet she ardently desired the holy Viaticum; and whenever they spoke to her of God her reason returned. The physician recommended their trying an unconsecrated host, and she succeded in swallowing it. At four in the evening, after she had been twenty-two hours in agony, the holy Viaticum was brought. Sister Mary Francis of Sales must herself describe what followed, "When they brought me our Lord," she writes, "I could neither see the priests, nor the sisters, nor the lights. I only knew I was going to communicate. As soon as I had received the holy Viaticum, I became conscious of myself and of my state. I felt my body burning all over. I understood that I had been very near death, and said so to the Superioress. Our Lord, after having shown me the state from which he was drawing me, said to me interiorly: *'It is I who can and will heal thee.'* I said to him *'Fiat'*; and I could not have said anything else, for I had no other feeling than to leave him to act. From the instant our Lord said this to me, a great change seemed to be working in all my side; my heart seemed to return and resume its place, but with a movement so violent that it frightened me. Yet not finding it followed by any suffering, and a feeling of ease coming over my whole frame, I perceived myself to be cured; so effectively and thoroughly. I had no more wish to make known this favor than I had previously had to receive it; however, after half or three quarters of an hour of thanksgiving, I told it to our Mother Superioress, and my countenance also spoke for me, for it had regained its natural appearance. I asked for something to drink, and drank without difficulty. They offered me something to eat, and I ate some soup with great pleasure. I walked about that same evening. My legs, which up to that time had been so much swollen, especially near the left foot, which was itself much diseased, had returned to their ordinary state, as well as my side. The cautery which I had over my heart was healed. I slept well all night. I breakfasted at five the next morning. At six the physician came, astonished at the state he found me in, instead of being dead. He examined me with great care, and said to me: 'Madam, you seem to me like one from the other world'. Ever since, I have been able to go up and down stairs, which I could not do for ten months before; I can lie on either side; I can use my left arm as well as my right. In short I am in perfect health, and able to follow all the duties of the community. Glory be to God, Glory to Mary!"

I will add the conclusion of the interesting document from which I have given these extracts.

"All these depositions having been received:

"Considering the certificate of the Messrs. Bruté, who attest:

"1. That the cure of Sister Mary Francis of Sales could not have been affected by the remedies employed, which were all in vain;

"2. That the sufferer had been reduced to the last agony;

"3. That they had given up employing remedies;

"4. That the cure was instantaneous;

"5. That the cure has now lasted for four months;

"Considering, likewise, the account drawn up by the sufferer herself;

"Likewise the deposition of the Abbé Corvaisier (the Chaplain):

"We have judged that the cure of Sister Mary Francis of Sales was wrought in a manner altogether extraordinary, and beyond the laws of physiology and pathology, and we have permitted the Mother Superioress, in consequence, to make known the facts above related, as well as to deliver copies of the present *procés-verbal*, to persons interested in knowing them.

Signed by

MM. Frain, Vicar-General, Superior;

The Abbe Corvaisier, Chaplain of the Visitation;

Bruté, Sen., Bruté, Jun.; The Physicians; **Sisters Mary Teresa**, Superioress;

Mary Elizabeth Bassi, Assistant;

Mary Pauline, Infirmarian;

Mary de Chantal;

Mary Francis of Sales;

Louisa Frances;

Stephana de Gonzaga.

The present *procés-verbal* was seen and approved by us, the Bishop of Rennes, the 2nd of August, 1849.

G. Bishop of Rennes

It is worthy of notice, that scarcely any of the miraculous cures of which I have given these brief accounts occurs at the time when the sick person looked for it. It is also deserving of remark, that many of the cures take place about four o'clock in the evening; this seems to have some relation with the time of the conclusion of the Apparition, which, as the children suppose, began between two and three o'clock. The reader will not fail to observe, that they have the most intimate relation with novenas and invocations of our Lady of La Salette and with the use of the water from what is so truly called the miraculous fountain.

(For futher information on the miracles obtained through the intercession of our Lady of La Salette, see Bishop Giray of Cahor's - "Les Miracles de La Salette," in two volumes.)

CHAPTER XIV

CONCLUSION

"He who is mighty hath done great things to me, and holy is his name."

Holy Mother

What thou didst sing with all thy prophetic soul on the mountains of Judea, thou hast made manifest on the mountain of La Salette. There was seen the shadow of thy brightness, tempered for mortal eyes to look upon, and the sun grew pale before it. There thou didst reveal thy maternal power with Jesus, and thy maternal love for us. There thou didst choose poor children out of all the world, two simple cowherds, to be the apostles of thy motherly pity and thy motherly love; and thou hast kept them in their simplicity. Thou wert found in the fields where they lay at midday; thou art honored where thy footsteps stood. Thy heavenly tears were for Jesus dishonored. The grief on thy face is for the many children, who abandon His grace, and who turn their backs upon His holy law. Alas! thou hast come to warn us how thy compassionate intercession with Jesus is bound up and restrained by the indifference of thy children. Jesus has almost exhausted His mercy, and thou hast almost exhausted intercession. Oh Mother of mercy, compelled by the love to be the messenger of vengeance, as a last resource thou hast come thyself to plead with us, and to move us by that voice of sweet and motherly tenderness. Thou hast come in the clear noonday, and hast found a world that was already dark, blind with sin, and dark with ingratitude. Thou hast revealed to us that deluge of calamities which hangs in the clouds above our heads; those last and most frightful mercies which, unless they repent, God has in store for His erring people. What does all this signify, but that without the co-operation of our wills, God cannot save us, and all thy prayers cannot help us with Him?

But He who is mighty has done great things for us through thee. Through thee He gave us His own eternal and well-beloved Son. In thee He gave us the perfect example of a pure, holy, and immaculate creature, loving Him perfectly, by the life of His Holy Spirit, which dwelt within thee. And from that dreadful Cross, whilst drowning death and sin in His great agony, Jesus the Son of God, Jesus, the Child of thy Womb, whilst He brought us back from death to life, gave us thee for our Mother and protectress. We have no mother in heaven but thee. The saints are our brothers and our sisters, and they love us well, and pray for us much; but they have not the mother's power with Jesus; they have not the mother's love for us. Jesus gave thee those maternal rights to exercise for us; Jesus gave us those claims to look as children up to thee, when, with those dying words He said to that one beloved child who stood there for us all: *"Son, behold thy Mother!"*

And, on the Holy Mountain which thou hast chosen, thou hast shown once more a mother's love and a mother's power: a mother's power with Jesus and a mother's love for us. Thou hast made eloquent the tongues of thy children.Thy power has been made manifest through their weakness. In thy Sanctuary the graces of thy Son, inclined over to thy prayers, have drawn those multitudes to repentance and conversion, and have filled them with peace and joy in the Holy Ghost, thy heavenly spouse. The miraculous waters of thy ever-flowing fountain are but a figure and a sign of that fountain of grace, that loving Heart of thy Divine Son, which ever flows; and which flows so abundantly at the voice of thy pleading from thy chosen Sanctuary, upon all who call upon His name through thee. Thou hast peopled the desert; thou has made the solitude to flourish; thou art the joyful Mother of . many repentant children. Health of the sick, Comfortress of the afflicted, Help of Christians, Reconciler of sinners, Joy of the pilgrim, pray for us who have recourse to thee.

> **Exert a Mother's care,**
> **And us thy children own;**
> **To Him convey our prayer,**
> **Who chose to be thy Son.**

Mary is inseparable from Jesus, and the glory of Mary is the glory of Jesus; her power the power of Jesus. Jesus is the life of all who live; Mary, our better Eve, is the mother of all the living. She exercises a mother's solicitude and a mother's ministry with a mother's love. If there is an earthly ministry there is also a heavenly ministry. Of the angels St. Paul says, that "they are all ministering spirits, sent to minister for those who shall receive the inheritance of salvation." And David says, "He has given His angels charge over thee." And the Saints have profited men more in Heaven than they ever did them service on earth. And the Church says in her prayer for the feast of the holy Archangel, the prince and leader of the heavenly hosts that God has constituted the ministry both of angels and of men *in wonderful order*. As a king exercises his power through ministers in many grades and orders, gives them power of interceding with him, makes them the channels of his favor in the degree in which they approach him, and exalts thereby his majesty and power; so Heaven's eternal King exalts His holy ones in power, and gives them a resemblance to Him, not only as He is holy, but also as He is mighty. They are seated on the thrones of His power. But at the right hand of Jesus, Queen of angels and of saints, is Mary, the fairest, the purest, and the most holy of that mighty host; exercising a mother's power, and full to perfection of a mother's love. If Michael, at the head of the heavenly hosts, was the chief protector of the Hebrew Church, Mary was not as yet upon her throne by the side of Jesus; Michael rules the angels, Mary all the choirs of the blessed. When she prays, they all pray in her company; when she lifts up her voice in supplication, they all extend their hands. If Abraham, by his justice, withheld the hand of God; if Moses, by his meekness, stayed back His avenging arm; Mary, by her love, restrains His justice when His mercy seems no longer to endure. Jesus sees the motive in her which He cannot find in us. Moved by those two great loves — the love of Jesus and the love of us — she prays and pleads with an irresistible power. And God loves to be overcome by the solicitude and love of that holiest of creatures, that most immaculate of beings.

The Apparition of our Mother on the mountain of La Salette is not the publication of a new doctrine, but of a new grace. It is a revelation of the love and pity which reigns in Heaven for us. God is exceedingly angry with His sinful chldren. The hands of Jesus are heavy with the accumulation of millions of ingratitudes. His Mother pleads earnestly for her children. Like Rachel, she weeps because they are not. The cruel enemy has slain their souls. Blasphemies abound. Churches mourn their widowhood. Men come not to the fountains of grace. Mary comes and proclaims these sad truths to France, at the very time that a new Pontiff rises in the pulpit of Rome, and opening his mouth for the first time, proclaims the same sad truths to the Roman people. Who does not remember the discourse of Pius IX in the church of Sant' Andrea della Valle? And as if he had in view the complaints of Mary at La Salette, in his encyclical letter to the Archbishops and Bishops of Italy of December, 1849, he urges the same subject anew in these remarkable words: Venerable brethren, in all things your cares and those of the priests, your co-operators, should tend especially to bring the faithful to conceive the greatest horror for crimes that cause scandal to our neighborhood. For you know that in various places the numbers have increased of those who dare publicly to *blaspheme the Saints of Heaven and even the most holy name of God; or who on the days set apart to God give themselves up to servile works, and open their shops; or who, in the presence of many despise the precepts of fasting and abstinence.* By the voice of your zeal, let the faithful be led to represent to themselves and seriously to consider the enormous gravity of sins of this kind, and the severe pains with which their authors will be punished."

And thus Mary complains with bitter sorrow, that a baptized, a Catholic people, a people consecrated to her, should live without God and without His Church. That in Heaven as on earth, hope for that people is perishing. Oh marvellous mercy of grace! All is at the gloomiest, and the deluge is impending, when, behold! the rainbow of peace appears in the heavens. Their gates are opened. A wondrous light is seen on that solitary Mountain, as Moses saw it in the bush, as Elias on Horeb, as the shepherds at Bethlehem. The sun is but as a taper before that wonderful brightness. It is the garment of the Mother of God. And, behold, she is seated on the fountain. She rises, she speaks, she carries the image of her Son upon her breast. He is crucified. She is weeping. And yet she is in glory. So the glorious God Himself was touched, before the deluge came "with sorrow of heart". Mary sorrows because the sorrows of Jesus come not near her children; she sorrows because they will not take His sorrows to their heart.

But what new garb is this of our Heavenly Mother? She no longer wears the white veil and the blue robe of the daughters of Nazareth. No, Mary comes not as a child of Nazareth, but as the Queen of Heaven. And not as she is beheld there, but as she may be apprehended here. It is in robes of white that she leads the virgin choirs in Heaven. And "the king's Mother stands at his right hand, in a garment of gold, surrounded with variety." She carries the symbols of the devotion of her clients as her ornaments. A rosary encircles her breast, a rosary crowns her head, rosaries sustain her feet. But around the roses so near her heart, there is a heavy chain — alas! the bondage of sinners. The chain of flowers and the chain of iron links — the devout souls and the sinful souls; Mary carries both in her loving remembrance; but one is joy, the other the anguish of that maternal heart. They are of many colors, those flowers, for she is encircled with variety and that variety is the varied devotion of her faithful children. But why does our Mother weep? Why does she carry a chain as if a bondswoman? And how does she suffer if the saints are past all sufferings? Mary's tears spring not from her own sufferings, they spring for our admonition. And if the blessed know no bondage of their own, we chain the freedom of their goodness towards us. We bind in captivity that wonderful efficacy of their prayers and of their services. Mary suffers restraint and coercion through our sins and indifference, in the exercise of her maternal intervention with her Son. "If my people will not submit, I am compelled to let go the arm of my

Son, it is so strong, so heavy, that I can no longer withhold it. How long do I suffer for you? If I would not have my Son abandon you, I am compelled to pray incessantly for you, and you make no account of it."

From the time that Melanie saw Mary the world had faded on her sight. If she has not sought the world, yet for the eight years past has the world been coming to her. But to the child of the vision of Mary the world has no beauty, no charm, no contentment. What St. Gregory the Great taught his deacon as a truth, she has experienced as a fact. And the eyes which beheld the glorious one from Heaven, finds the earthly creation divested of beauty, and shorn of power to attract her heart. Nothing is beautiful to those eyes which have seen the beauty of Mary. Nothing is brilliant to that sight which saw the splendor of her glory. Nothing is melodious to those ears which listened to her Heavenly voice. Her looks are lifted to the mountains whence her Mother came. And if such be the beauty, such the sweetness, such the glory of Mary, even as seen in her distress, and by the mortal eyes of a poor child, what is the beauty of Jesus, what His sweetness, and what His Glory, as seen by Mary herself, and by those blessed and immortal spirits, whose natures the light of glory has adapted to live in the vision of His infinite beauty and in the power of His endless glory; whose hearts the Spirit of eternal Charity has drawn into the sweetest embrace of His unbounded love.

All do not receive this Heavenly vision, nor these words of Mary, and yet it is an enforcement of the Catholic truth. Still it is no part of "the Catholic faith, which, except a man believe faithfully and steadfastly, he cannot be saved." Like the counsel of our Lord, all do not receive it, but those to whom it is given. There is a faith which rests upon the doctrines of the Church, and content with that, looks not beyond. And there is a faith which is ever standing betwixt the borders of time and eternity, keenly alive with interest for every sound which is heard from the Heavens. There are souls, and faithful souls, who are little disposed to cultivate the supernatural beyond the beaten track.

There are others who are overcredulous, and who seize every rumor of things, professing to come from beyond this world, without much care or consideration for its evidence. Then, again, there are souls whose faith is dull and sluggish, because it is not cultivated with any degree of earnest prayer; souls whose faith rests more on habit than it lives by action. To such a believer it is a burden which he bears, perhaps somewhat painfully, perhaps with a certain sense of humiliation rather than of humility. It is not the animating principle which carries him through his everyday life. The cares of the world are uppermost with him, or pleasures absorb him, or he is vain of his knowledge, or proud of his reason, or human respect has taken hold of him, has entered within him, and holds his soul captive. This is a large class, and to them the report of news from Heaven, is comonly attended with more uneasiness than interest, and rather inclines to give trouble than to awaken or console. Not often in the case, because they are wisely prudent, and unwilling to commit themselves, but because the supernatural has no charms for them. The invisible world is remote from their minds and aloof from their affections. The foreign intelligence in which they delight is of another kind. Their souls have made no home, no affectionate friends in their spiritual country. They believe in miracles as a general point of faith, but would thank you not to bring them to their door. The last despatch from the seat of war is incomparably more interesting to them than the "great news" brought by the Mother of God from Heaven. The title of this book may deter many of that class from opening it. But it was never intended for them.

There is another class who will read this book, but who have an impression on their minds, that neither the Apparition of our Lady of La Salette, nor her warnings, nor her prophecy, regard us in this country — that they mainly refer to France — that at all events the second and the third commandments of God are not those which are the most neglected in England. Alas! let us all reflect a little upon what we know. England is full of blasphemies, and what before Heaven, is an English Sunday? What are the habits of our rude and ignorant poor?

What their language? and what their life on Sundays? Does it stop here? Look at the late census, and survey both town and country. The shops are closed and work ceases, but where are the great masses of the people? Is it to God they give themselves? How long will men confound cessation of business and the stopping of work, whatever be the motive, with observance of the Sunday? Then, let us turn nearer home, to our own poor people. How many scattered over the face of the country, without church or pastor, go to no Mass, and live without the observance of the Sunday? When there is a new mission commenced, where numbers beyond all anticipation are found, children of the faith have lived without the exercises of its duties. And then, for that vice for which Mary mourns, and which weighs down the arm of her son — "they swear and introduce the name of my Son."

Then, for the blasphemy — blasphemy against Jesus in His Holy Eucharist — blasphemy against Jesus in His Holy Sacrifice. Our sovereigns are not crowned without it. Our peers enter not the Senate without it. Our representatives enter into parliament with it on their lips. Terrible oaths in which God is called to witness against Himself. They form a part of our laws, they are an element of our Constitution. Then add to these blasphemies those others against the Mother of our Lord, and against His saints, those against the other sacraments and against holy things, and those against the Church of God. How much of this do we continually hear from members of the legislature, and from officials of all degrees. Let us consider those blasphemies, more dreadful still, which are uttered in a sort of satanic fervor on platforms and in powerful associations. That active propagandism, those energetic organizations, all those hired instruments, upheld and sent forth, with no other object than to spread and promote these blasphemies, and to bring our poor to join in them with the yet deeper criminality of apostasy. Then consider that more horrible class of apostates, men driven from the sanctuaries which they have profaned by their crimes, going forth with the light of truth within them, however defiled, and gathering in this land for the mere price which is paid for their blasphemies. And they come and invent such blasphemies as hell alone can match in atrocity, and which, but for their hire, they would never think of inventing, nor of giving utterance to.

Next consider how widely our literature is imbued with abuse and denial of the things of God. How the crime of blasphemy, not coarsely, not vulgarly, but deeply and efficaciously penetrates into so many of our books of science. How it spreads through so many of our periodicals. How loudly and how vehemently it is heard in vast numbers of our newspapers.

Consider again, our English Sunday with reference to this most melancholy subject, and those thousands of pulpits, from which, to speak against Jesus in His Holy Eucharist, in His Holy Sacrifice, in His other Sacraments, in His Blessed Mother, in His Saints, in His Church, in His Vicar on earth, is the entertainment mingled with the invocation of God, and furnished for the guidance of so many of our countrymen.

There may be ignorance behind all this blasphemy, and to an undefinable extent there is, blind and dreadful ignorance. But that unhallowed temper which is so widely exhibited can never be called invincible. The excitement, the unscrupulousness, the fierce passion, the bitter and turbulent zeal with which these blasphemies come out from the mouths of so many of our countrymen, are the sad and too sensible proof if they could see or would reflect, that they are not acting with that spirit of God, which is peaceful, mild, patient, charitable; but that they are contending against the Holy Spirit of peace. It is the terrible spectacle of the Pharisees and Sadducees before our Lord that is renewed in this age against His institutions, His doctrines, and His saints. But let us suppose, however impossible the supposition may be, that men, and men baptized, and acting under the impression that they have insurmountable conviction, can deny, and insult, and defile the truths of God and the facts of His holy religion, after they have been proclaimed to them and heard by them, with as

much ease and peace of conscience as they may deal in a like spirit
with whatever is in itself intrinsically false and without any relation-
ship with their own souls; even then, what a spectacle to God and to
all good souls is a vast and agitated multitude of men, blindly ignorant,
and passionately blaspheming the truths of Heaven and the sacraments of grace, the most divine gifts of God and the holiest fruits of
the love of Jesus.

After thus considering what England is, and especially what an
English Sunday is — say, whether there is no voice for us in La Salette.
Whether we do not require to practise expiations and atonements.
Whether we have no need of such a Confraternity as that of Our Lady
of La Salette, Reconciler of Sinners, for the reparation of blasphemy
and the abuse of the Sunday. Whether of all expiatory devotions it is
not the one most needed, most adapted to our wants and to our
circumstances.

That heavenly voice was undoubtedly addressed to France
immediately and in the first instance. It has already carried both its
warnings and its blessings into countries more remote. But La Salette
is intimately associated with the Catholic Church in this country. It has
already caused much prayer to be said for England. Twice a day the
missioners of La Salette invite the pilgrims, as they arrive, to offer up
their prayers for England. Twice a day in that holy Sanctuary are
prayers in public offered up in our behalf. I am not without grave
reason for believing that a part of one of those mysterious secrets has
reference to the future of the Church of England. I do not now refer to
a statement recently published, for I am satisfied, through my own
examinations, that in part of its details on this subject, however
accurate in others, there is some mistake; and yet I venture to affirm
that I have been able to put together, from different points, evidence
sufficient in its construction to satisfy my own mind, that Mary spoke
of England, and in words that intimate a day of consolation in some
future time. I cannot but join my impression of such an intimation with

those continuous prayers which she has moved her children on her Holy Mountain to offer for our country. And it is with the hope of inducing pious Catholics in England to join their devotions with those of our brethren on the Continent, and with those of our Lady's pilgrims, more fervently and more abundantly; and to give them a motive for invoking our Lady of La Salette with more devotion and more confidence, that I have been led to give this expression to the convictions which I have imbibed.

Let me conclude with the words of a very great personage, which, though spoken in private, have found their way to the public ear:

"The Pilgrimage of La Salette is Authentic and Full of the Future."

APPENDIX

Note A — Transportation

Transportation facilities to the Sanctuary of La Salette are much different at present to those described by Bishop Ullathorne in his first and second chapters. Arriving at Genoble by rail from Paris, the pilgrim today can avail himself of motor bus service direct to the Basilica and the site of the Apparition. There is, also, train service from Grenoble to Corps where busses are available for the journey up the mountain to the Shrine, located approximately six thousand feet above sea level.

Note B — The Basilica and Shrine

With offerings received from the faithful in all parts of the world, a magnificent basilica in Roman-Byzantine style, and two vast hospices, were built within a comparatively short time. The material employed, for the most part, was black, unpolished marble, quarried from the side of the towering Mount Gargas. The cost of construction was approximately three million francs — $700,000. In 1890 twenty side-chapels were added to the basilica, and the hotels were also enlarged to accomodate the throngs of pilgrims. The basilica with its numerous and rich capels, and its twin towers that seem to vie in majesty with the surrounding mountain peaks never fails to excite the enthusiastic admiration of the visitor. It can accommodate three thousand persons, and yet it is too small for the numbers that assemble on feast days to honor the spot made sacred by the presence of the Mother of God.

The walls are literally hidden under marble slabs and ex-voto offerings, which give eloquent testimony of the many favors obtained through the intercession of our Lady of La Salette.

The stately main altar, surmounted by the beautiful statue of the crowned Virgin, placed under an arch of gold and silver hearts, all ex-voto offerings; the pulpit, a masterpiece of sculpture, the gift of the grateful people of Belgium; the superb organ whose majestic tones first vibrated through the Basilica, when the statue of our Lady of La Salette was solemnly crowned by Cardinal Guibert of Paris; a richly embroidered canopy; a ciborium studded with diamonds, a souvenir of the Golden Jubilee of the apparition; a magnificent diadem that served for the crowning of the statue of our Lady of La Salette, constitute some of the riches of the Sanctuary, and excite the admiration of visitors.

In the midst of all this splendor, and guarded with jealous care is the simple, rough stone which served as the humble throne of the Blessed Mother, on the hallowed day of the apparition.

The actual site of the apparition in a small ravine below the Basilica is marked out by beautiful bronze statues representing the three phases of the Apparition — the Weeping Mother as She was first discovered by the children seated on a stone, the Blessed Virgin delivering Her message to the two young witnesses, and finally Her return to Heaven. The Stations of the Cross are erected along the path traced out by the Mother of God, and this devotion is one of the favorite practices of pilgrims on a visit to La Salette.

Note C - The Witnesses after the Apparition

The favored witnesses of the Apparition fulfilled their mission well. The celestial Messenger had ordered them to make her teachings known to all her people, and it seems that really the voice of the *Beautiful Lady* has reached throughout the whole world by means of these two little shepherds.

To some, however, their lives do not seem to have been in keeping with the great favor they had received, and thus the inference is drawn that this fact weakens somewhat the proofs of the Apparition. This objection, however, is rather specious. Indeed the two witnesses, as far as we know, did not become eminent for their sanctity, but we do know that both lived well enough to deserve to be proposed as models for most of their accusers, Melaine having always enjoyed a reputation for sincere piety, while Maximin had always been a good practical Catholic in spite of his defects.

But did the Apparition really oblige them to attain a greater perfection of sanctity than others? We would not venture to say so. The favor they received was not for *them* especially, but for *all*, and we may add, more for *others* than for *themselves*. Maximin used to give rather striking answers to his accusers, on this score; here is one of them: "I saw the Blessed Virgin once, but as for you, you have not only seen, but received our Lord Himself perhaps a hundered times, and do you think that this favor, though more common, is not infinitely greater?"

The lives of the two witnesses of the Apparition have been, we may say, lives of struggle and suffering. Providence, it seems, could allot nothing better to those who had contemplated the Mother of God sunk in deepest grief, and to whom had been confided the secret of heavy chastisement hanging over sinful mankind.

We have already seen how Melanie became a Sister of Providence. Forced to leave France, for a while, on account of the Apparition — of which, it is said, the Government of Napoleon III was afraid — she went to England, where she entered a monastery at Darlington. After her return to France in 1860, she was admitted into the convent of the Sisters of the Compassion, at Marseilles. Then Mgr. Petagna, Bishop of Castellamare, took her to Italy, to found a community of teaching Sisters, but the plan was not carried out, and at the death of her protector, Melanie returned to the South of France, where she lived with her mother, at Cannet, near Cannes. After the death of her mother, which occurred in 1890, Melanie lived alternately in France and Italy. During the last years of her life she made several pilgrimages to the shrine of La Salette, which always remained so dear to her. She never ceased to consider herself the apostle of the Great Event of 1846. And

Bishop Fava, answering a newspaper which had published a supposed retraction made by Melanie, could write:

"Melanie, whom I questioned at Castellamare, about two months ago, would seal with her blood the account she has given of the Apparition, and to which she has always adhered."

In June, 1904, Melanie went to reside at Altamura, a little town in Southern Italy, where she enjoyed, for a time, the kind hospitality of an honorable and Christian family. Here she lived a life of meditation and prayer, assisting at daily Mass.

On the morning of December 15th, 1904, she was missed at church; and after investigation by the authorities of the town she was found dead in her room. Though her death was sudden, she was well prepared to meet her God by a life of union with the crucified Savior and His sorrowful Mother.

The Bishop of Altamura presided at her funeral, which was attended by a large concourse of people.

Maximin had a still more troubled career. After a brief sojourn at the little seminary of le Rondeau, he went to several ecclesiastical colleges, but because of his fickle character, he did not succeed in his studies. Afterwards we find him successively a medical student, a Papal Zouave, a Government official in Paris, a merchant, etc. Finally he returned to Corps, his native town, and remained there until his death.

In 1864, Maximin felt the first symptoms of what was to be a fatal malady. At the close of 1874 he appeared to be in a hopeless condition. Seeing that his death was near, he wished to go to the Holy Mountain for the last time, in order to pray to the Mother of Sorrows. It was on the 4th of November, 1874, he made this last ascent to La Salette. The next morning, after having spent several hours in prayer in the Basilica, he directed his steps to the miraculous fountain. He seemed to be wholly taken up with the sight of that blessed spot, once the witness of the great Event. Several times he walked the path trodden by the *Beautiful Lady*, and seemed never to tire gazing upon the place where the Apparition had disappeared in a halo of light.

The Sisters of La Salette lavished the tenderest care on their invalid visitor. They had recently taken the place of the Sisters of Providence at La Salette, and hence had never heard from his own lips a recital of the Apparition. So they asked him for this favor now. He cheerfully complied with their request, first in the Convent, and afterwards, on the place of the Apparition, in the presence of many pilgrims. Never had he spoken with so much emotion. His words carried with them every mark of truthfulness, and his countenance seemed to the witnesses, to be transfigured. For the last time he was fulfilling the mission given him by Our Lady, in making known to her people the solemn warnings of 1846.

After gazing for a long time with deep sadness at the sacred Mountain, where the Mother of God had appeared to him in such splendor, he went back to Corps.

Misery and want fell to his lot. It would seem that God wished to make him expiate his past dreams of ambition. A few days before his death he asked for the last Sacraments, and received them with great fervor and piety. He died on March 1, 1875.

He was endowed with superior intelligence, but had a changeable disposition, which he failed to control, and that in itself accounts for his want of success. However, in spite of his fickleness, he was faithful to his mission, even amongst the greatest temptations of the world. We have already remarked that he led a good life, attended faithfully to all his Christian duties, and moreover went to the Sacraments every month.

Fearing lest he might in future be accused of having withdrawn his evidence on the fact of La Salette, he left a written testimony of it.

This is what we read in his will: "In the name of the Father, and of the Son, and of the Holy Ghost. Amen. I believe all that the Holy

Roman Catholic Church teaches, all the dogmas defined by our Holy Father the Pope, the august and infallible Pius IX. I firmly believe, even at the cost of my life, in the celebrated Apparition of the Most Blessed Virgin, on the Mountain of La Salette, which occurred on the 19th of September, 1846; and which Apparition I have defended by word, writing, and suffering. After my death, let no man pretend that I have retracted, or that he has heard me retract the great event of La Salette, for in deceiving himself, he would deceive the world."

That declaration, made as it was at the very threshold of eternity, is of prime importance. People do not lie at that supreme hour. Supposing — what cannot be supposed — that he had persisted till death in giving a false account of the miracle, his first care at the approach of death, and at the thought of the God he was about to meet, would have been to strike his breast and say: I have sinned against truth! And had human respect kept him from making such a confession, he would have at least remained silent; but as it was he proclaimed anew with wonderful energy the reality of the Apparition.

Note D - The Prophecies and Their Fulfillment

Historical records strikingly bear out the fact of the fulfillment of these dire predictions made by our Blessed Mother at La Salette, events which the two ignorant children were in nowise able to foresee. Certainly famine came to France and many other countries in a few years after the apparition. The French newspaper "Constitutionnel" in March 1856, commented: "Though a complete list of the deaths for the year 1855 has not yet been brought to our knowledge, by the results already known, we are led to believe that the year will show an extraordinary increase of mortality, of at least eighty thousand persons, whose deaths were caused by the continuation of the high price of food." This "high price of food" meant simply that nearly a hundred thousand people had died of starvation. The same newspaper gave the number of the famine victims in 1854, as sixty thousand. In 1856, the number rose higher still. So, "the high price of food," to use the words of the "Constitutionnel", caused at least 250,000 deaths from 1854 to 1856, in France alone. And to say that, during these three years, as many as one million persons became victims of starvation throughout Europe, is to fall short of the reality.

As to Ireland, where the famine was severest, we have only to read the speech of Queen Victoria, at the opening of the English Parliament, January 19, 1847, to see that there, the very year of the apparition, the loss of the potato crop was the cause of cruel suffering and of a terrible increase of the mortality rate.

Note E - The Secrets

The content of the secrets confided to the two children by our Blessed Mother of La Salette has always intrigued human curiosity. Beyond what is mentioned in the work of Archbishop Ullathorne little else is authentically known of the secrets. In a private audience, the Very Reverend Father S. M. Giraud, at that time Superior General of the Missionaries of our Lady of La Salette, asked His Holines Pope Pius IX, if he might know something of the secrets. The Holy Father answered: "You wish to know the secrets of La Salette? Well, here are the secrets of La Salette: Unless you do penance, you shall all perish."

Numerous books and pamphlets have been published from time to time on this subject, some of which even claimed to reproduce the complete text of Melanie's secret. Efforts to interpret the secrets in connection with current political affairs, and other more or less fantastic commentaries on the supposed secrets tended to bring odium on the whole Apparition and discredit its supernatural and devotional character.

Such publications naturally aroused a storm of criticism and on several occasions the Roman Congregations condemned books of this type, supposedly containing the secrets of La Salette.

Chief among the decisions of Rome on the matter is the decree emanating from the Sacred Congregation of the Holy Office on December 21, 1915.

To those who were not familiar with the question, that decree sounded as though it were a condemnation of the Apparition itself. Nothing, however, is further from the truth.The decree reproduced here will convince anyone that Rome made a clear distinction between what was circulated as the Secrets of La Salette and the devotion of our Lady of La Salette.

The Decree is as follows:

"It has come to the knowledge of the Supreme Congregation that there are still persons, even ecclesiastics, who in spite of the answers and decisions of the Sacred Congregation itself, continue by books, pamphlets, and articles published in periodicals, whether signed or anonymous, to discuss the question of the Secrets of La Salette, its various texts, its adaptations to our present times or to the future — and these, not only without the approbation of their Bishops, but even in spite of their express prohibition. In order that these abuses, which are harmful to true piety, and seriously attack ecclesiastical authority, may be repressed, the same Sacred Congregation orders the faithful of all countries to abstain from treating and discussing this said question, under whatsoever pretext or form, either in books, pamphlets, or articles signed or anonymous, or in any other way."

After specifying the penalties to be inflicted on the transgressors, the Decree concludes: "This Decree is not, however, contrary to the devotion to the Blessed Virgin invoked and known under the title of Reconciler of La Salette."

Given at Rome, at the Palace of the Holy Office, Decmeber 21, 1915.

(signed)
Louis Castellano
Notary S. R. et U. I.

Note F - Missionaries of Our Lady of La Salette

The congregation of the Missionaries of our Lady of La Salette was founded in Grenoble, France in 1852,the Bishop of the Diocese at the time being the Most Reverend Philibert de Bruillard. It was intended, the Bishop wrote in his Pastoral, to be "like the Shrine itself, an eternal monument, a perpetual remembrance of the merciful Apparition of Mary." In the beginning it consisted merely of a chosen body of priests, living in community life, and providing for the spiritual needs of pilgrims visiting the Shrine. For twenty-four years the new Community remained diocesan in character, under the authority of the Bishop of Grenoble, with a provision Constitution.

In 1876 the Congregation passed from diocesan to pontifical status, and in 1890 it received the formal approval of His Holiness, Leo XIII. The Constitutions of the Missionaries of our Lady of La Salette were given definite approbation by the Sovereign Pontiff Pius XI, June 7th, 1926.

The special end of the Congregation, as outlined in the Constitutions, is the Apostolate: "to combat the crimes of the day", especially those crimes deplored by our Blessed Mother on the mountain of La Salette: neglect of Holy Mass and prayer, profanation of the Lord's Day and of His Sacred Name, and the lack of submission to the laws of God and of the Church. The aim of the Apparition of the Blessed Virgin, and consequently of the Congregation instituted to propagate her teachings, is a revival of true practical Christianity in the daily life of the faithful. To promote this end the Missionaries "preach missions and retreats, found and direct Apostolic Schools, take charge of shrines, and particularly that of La Salette, the cradle and Mother-House of the Congregation, and devote themselves to foreign missions" (Constitutions, Part I, C. I. a. I, n. 2, 3).

After the early formative years the Congregation grew rapidly and soon established houses in several dioceses of France. The religious persecution in France, in 1901, obliged the pioneer members to take refuge in other countries, and so in the Providence of God contributed to the spread of the Community. New Houses were established in Italy, Belgium, Poland, Switzerland, the United States, England, Canada, Madagascar, Brazil, Burma, Argentina, Philippines, Africa and the Duchy of Lichtenstein. This universal character of the Congregation was apparent as early as 1879 when the first Missionaries labored in Norway under Monsignor Bernard Bernard, Prefect Apostolic to Norway and Lapland, and himself a Missionary of La Salette.

At the present time the Missionaries of our Lady of La Salette have over six hundred candidates preparing for the Holy Priesthood and the religious life in the sixteen Scholasticates, Novitiates and preparatory Colleges conducted by them in these different countries.

The rapid growth of the Congregation in recent years necessitated its division into provinces. With the approval of the Holy See, after the General Chapter of the Order in 1932, four Provinces were created: the Province of our Lady of La Salette comprising the residence of France, the preparatory college in Tournai, Belgium and the Vicariate of Antsirabé in Madagascar; the Province of our Lady of Seven Dolors which includes the residences in the United States, England and Burma; the Province of the Immaculate Conception in Brazil, and the Province of St. Stanislaus in Poland. To these have recently been added a Province in Switzerland comprising the Swiss-German residences and a preparatory college in the Principality of Lichtenstein, and the Province of the Immaculate Heart of Mary, Enfield, N. H., with a preparatory college, novitiate and major seminary.

The first Amercan foundation dates from 1892 when the Missionaries were received into the Diocese of Hartford by Bishop McMahon, who placed at their disposal his former residence. A large monastery was built in 1894, in Hartford, Connecticut, which has since become the center of the activities of the Congregation in America.

The American Provinces now count 3 major seminaries, located at Ipswich, Mass., Attleboro, Mass. and Olivet, Ill. In addition they have three novitiates, located at Bloomfield, Conn.; Brewster, Mass. and Olivet, Ill. and five preparatory Juniorates for junior students, located in Hartford, Conn., Millford, Iowa; Jefferson City, Mo., Enfield, N. H. and Olivet, Ill.

Besides these institutions, the Congregation has houses in the States of Connecticut, New York, Massachusetts, New Hampshire, Michigan, Iowa, West Virginia, Louisiana, Texas, Mississippi and Illinois.

In 1905 the Missionaries extended their labors to the Prairie Provinces of Northwest Canada, where vast mission fields were confided to their care. As these became self-supporting they were relinquished in favor of the secular clergy. However, the Polish Fathers still serve the Missions of Beausejour, Elma, and Ladywood in the Province of Manitoba.

In 1928 the first American Missionaries established themselves in England, on the invitation of the Most Reverend Arthur Doubleday D. D., Bishop of Brentwood, taking over the care of St. Peter's parish in Dagenham, Essex.

In 1937, the Province of Our Lady of Seven Dolors opened a new mission in Arakan, Burma. Five missionaries started the work there in that year to be joined by several more contingents in the years following. Recently the Mission was declared a Prefecture Apostolic with Right Rev. Msgr. Thomas Newman, M. S. as Prefect Apostolic of Akyab. — At present there are 11 missionaries working there and two have sacrificed their lives.

As auxiliaries of the Congregation a new Community of Sisters was founded in 1937 by the Very Reverend Celestin Crozet, M. S., former Superior General, called the Missionary Sisters of our Lady of La Salette. The aim of these Missionary Sisters is also the Apostolate, and they devote themselves to the corporal and spiritual works of mercy both in home and foreign lands. Already their numbers have increased rapidly, and at the Mother-House and Novitiate which is located at Soissons, France, there are found among the candidates preparing for the religious life and mission work representatives from England, Ireland, the United States, Canada, Poland, Switzerland, and Italy.

Note G - Rome and La Salette

It is easy to infer what the Holy See thinks of La Salette from the last words of Archbishop Ullathorne in Chapter XII, but this little book would not appear complete, nor satisfactory, unless we offered a few more explanations.

In 1875, Monsignor Paulinier was appointed to the Archbishopric of Besancon, and was succeeded in the See of Grenoble by Monsignor Fava. The latter had been previously Bishop of La Martinique (West Indies), where he had spread the devotion of our Lady of La Salette. As a reward for his zeal, it would seem, our Blessed Mother chose him to be the guardian of her privileged Mountain, and to further the work of beautifying her cherished Sanctuary of La Salette.

Indeed, there was something still wanting to complete the glory of our Lady's shrine. Her Basilica had not been consecrated, nor had the Roman Pontiff given the Indult for the Crowning of the Statue of our Lady of La Salette. But in 1879, both favors were granted by our Holy Father Leo XIII, at the request of Monsignor Fava.

The consecration of the Church took place on August 20th, 1879, and the solemn Coronation of our Lady on the next day. We give here a brief description of these great solemnities which lasted several days.

On the 18th of August Monsignor Bernard, Prefect Apostolic
of Norway and of the Missions of the North, arrived on the Holy
Mountain. In the evening the Basilica could hardly accommodate the
number of pilgrims who had come for the occasion. The Prelate
ascended the pulpit and made a moving appeal to all present to become
apostles of our Lady's teachings. We quote a part of his discourse:

"One of the witnesses of the Apparition is dead, the other is a
humble woman who cannot publish throughout the world the maternal admonitions of Mary; and yet this solemn message must be made
known to all her people. This is why everyone here present should
strive to become an apostle, and preach that message. It is also in order
to attain that end more surely that Divine Providence has made La
Salette a center of apostleship, where Mary's Missionaries must
enrich their souls with her teachings and whence they should go forth
to announce them throughout the whole world."

On the 19th, pilgrims flocked to La Salette from all parts. The
streets of Grenoble were thronged with so many strangers, that the
intelligent and enterprising Committee was unable to provide means
of conveyance for all the pious travellers. Many were obliged to
discontinue their pilgrimage, while others walked fifty-three miles
from Grenoble to La Salette.

On the evening of the same day the insignia of the Basilica were
displayed for the first time. They were composed of the Papal colors,
and of the coat of arms of our Lady of La Salette, on which is engraved
the newly conferred title: "Minor Basilica of our Lady of La Salette."

As the sun disappeared beyond the horizon, the summits of the
surrounding mountains began to look like dark phantoms in the
twilight. Then, suddenly, the joyous peals of the bells announced the
approach of the Bishops who had been invited for this solemn
occasion. The pilgrims, carrying lighted torches, went to meet them.
The Basilica and its surroundings were brilliantly illuminated. Cardi-

nal Guibert of Paris, Monsignor Pichenot, Archbishop of Chambery, Monsignor Paulinier, Archbishop of Besancon, and Monsignor Fava, Bishop of Grenoble, headed the procession. After them came Monsignor Mermillod, afterwards Cardinal, Bishop of Geneva and Lausanne, Monsignor Cotton, Bishop of Valence, Monsignor de Terris, Bishop Frejus, Monsignor Robert, Bishop of Marseilles, Monsignor Bonnet, Bishop of Viviers, Monsignor Delaunoy, Bishop of Aire, and the Right Reverend Dom Antoine, Abbot of the Trappe of Chambaran.

The procession halted under an arch of triumph. There, Monsignor Fava, addressing Cardinal Guibert and his colleagues in the Episcopacy, extended to them a cordial welcome. He expressed regret that Cardinal Desprez of Toulouse was not present, owing to illness. Then the procession advanced to the place of the Apparition, and after a short prayer entered the Basilica. It was with difficulty that the procession of Prelates made their way through the dense throngs.

Then Monsignor Cotton of Valence ascended the pulpit and addressed the assemblage of pilgrims, telling them in a few touching words what should be their feelings on entering the Sanctuary of the Mother of Sorrows.

The next morning, Monsignor Paulinier consecrated the Basilica. During the afternoon, Vespers were sung in the open air. It would be impossible to describe this part of the day's ceremony. Never did a choir render with grander tones or livelier faith the Psalms of David. Upwards of five hundred priests and over twenty-five thousand people were present.

At the close of the Vespers, the powerful voice of Monsignor de Terris was raised to defend the supernatural against the taunts and attacks of unbelievers. Speaking of the miracles of La Salette, he said: "Never did the truth of any miracle meet with such rage and evident bad faith! What falsities have the scoffing unbelievers not tried to allege, when the two children said that they saw, in that vale, upon

which I now gaze so delightfully, things which they did not understand, and heard a language hitherto unknown to them, every word of
which they nevertheless repeated without any contradiction, in spite
of the searching and embarrassing questions of thousands of believers
and unbelievers? And since then, what insidious reports have been
circulated in the papers! what insults, what scorns at the miracle of the
Holy Mountain!" Mgr. de Terris, then, begged leave to cite a particular circumstance of the Apparition, a circumstance at which the
opponents would not have smiled as a pilgrim did, had they happened
to read the discourse of the Bishop of Fréjus. "While Maximin and
Melanie stood there surrounded by the radiance of the Apparition and
awestruck with astonishment, not being able to understand the Blessed
Virgin's words, they began to question each other. Nearby stood
Maximin's dog, a vicious animal, and still he kept quiet. From that
day, the miracle has had its barkers, even among Christians; for some
there are who, unable to reason, are more unable still to remain silent;
and thus it will be to the end.

"To the insults and stupid denials of impiety an answer must be
given. The Episcopacy and the Clergy gave it in their teachings; they
expressed it in that strong positive language which belongs by right to
the Church, since it possesses the right to teach all truth. The Faithful,
on their side, protested by their confidence in our Lady of La Salette,
and by the outburst of the most touching piety. Was this sufficient?
No, we had to give a protestation as solemn as the insult had been
public, and which would go further than the ordinary teaching of the
Church, and the loyal faith of her children, a protestation which would
reach beyond the shadow of the Sanctuary, and beyond the privacy of
the family circle. Thus has France protested; thus has the Catholic
world protested by the solemn pilgrimages which so readily became
popular in our day; thus do we protest today in a striking manner, by
the consecration of a Basilica, and by the magnificent feats which now
attract the attention of all Christendom.

At 8 o'clock in the morning of the 21st, a general procession was formed and numerous banners floated in the breeze. Between the Clergy and the Bishops, appeared in a dazzling splendor the crown which the Delegate of the Sovereign Pontiff was going to place on the brow of the Virgin. An expert alone could fully appreciate the beauty of the countless gems that are placed in that masterpiece of art.

The procession, after many graceful windings, halted in front of a raised platform, on which an altar had been erected. Cardinal Guibert took his place at the foot of the altar, near the still unveiled statue of our Lady. Mass was then celebrated. Despite the large number of singers, the music was wonderfully harmonious and sweet. Towards the end of Mass, Mgr. Fava delivered an eloquent sermon, showing how, as Jesus Christ never sought His own glory, but that of His Heavenly Father, so in like manner, Mary the Mother of God never looked for *her* glory, but constantly aimed at procuring that of her Divine Son. It would seem, from all she has said at La Salette, that the main object of her Apparition there, was to urge the Faithful to repair and further the honor of Jesus Christ. She humbled herself for this end, in taking the appearance of a simple peasant woman. But the day of her triumph has come.

These few words give in substance the Bishop's beautiful discourse which was delivered with the skill of a master in the art of oratory. At the conclusion, the speaker was loudly applauded by his audience.

Cardinal Guibert then proceeded to crown the Virgin. The statue was unveiled. The assembled throng made the very mountains re-echo with shouts of joy, and after the hymn "O Gloriosa Virginum" had been sung, the Cardinal kneeling intoned the "Regina Coeli", which was immediately taken up by an enthusiastic people; and while the sweet "alleluiahs" rent the air, it almost seemed to the listeners, that they heard the Angels' thrilling hymns of praise before the throne of Mary in Heaven.

As soon as the singing ceased, the Cardinal placed the crown upon our Lady's brow. At that moment the bells of the Basilica rang out their joyous peals, while the cannon on the slope of Mount Gargas sent forth its mighty roar; but above all, like one great voice of praise rose the people's glorious cry: "Honor to our Lady of La Salette!" Then followed loud cheers for Leo XIII, Cardinal Guibert, Mgr. Fava, and all the Bishops present.

At Vespers on the same day, Mgr. Mermillod gave a discourse which deeply moved the congregation. All present were agreed that the renowned orator surpassed himself in eloquence on that occasion. Here is an extract from his speech: "In this Apparition, there are two things to be considered: a mountain upon which the Virgin descends, and shepherds to whom she speaks. A mountain! Does it not seem that mountains play a prominent part in the history of the world? Was it not on Mount Arrat that God stopped the ark that carried mankind? Was it not on Mount Sinai that God proclaimed His Law? Was it not on Mount Thabor that He revealed His Glory? Was it not on Mount Olivet that He wept, and on Calvary that He died? And was it not from that mountain, where He endured His agony, that He ascended into Heaven? Mountains appear and have always appeared to me to be the frontiers between God and man. God descends and man ascends to approach God. We read in history that, in ancient times, when two nations had been engaged in war, a mountain was often chosen as a place for signing a treaty of peace. Thus is La Salette the mountain chosen by God to make a treaty of peace with men."

Then with graceful tact, the eloquent Bishop of Geneva, knowing that his audience was almost entirely French, spoke of the predilection of God for their country. He showed how France had been twice providentially saved by two shepherdesses: St. Genevieve and Joan of Arc; and how in this country the Blessed Virgin by her Apparition seemed deeply interested in the welfare of this nation, whose influence for good and evil is felt throughout the whole world.

The Pontiff concluded by saying that after such manifestations of God's goodness, the hearts of the French people should be full of hope for the religious future of their beautiful Fatherland.

These splendid festivals at La Salette seemed to find an echo in the entire Catholic World. The telegrams and letters received at the Holy Mountain from all parts, and from every class of people, showed that hundreds of thousands were there in spirit. The Holy Father Leo XIII himself sent by telegram his blessing to the pilgrims. But this did not satisfy the promptings of his paternal heart; a few days afterwards he wrote to the Bishop of Grenoble:

"We were happy to learn, with what splendor and solemnity you carried out the ceremony of the Coronation of the Blessed Virgin, under the title of our Lady of La Salette, who is the object of such remarkable veneration in your diocese. Great has been our joy to know that a large concourse of the faithful accompanied by many Bishops, and honored by the presence of a Cardinal gave there admirable evidence of their piety and filial love towards the Blessed Virgin. This result is in part due to your apostolic zeal. We, therefore, congratulate you cordially, while giving due praise to your constant efforts to promote among the people an ardent love for the Immaculate Virgin. The love and devotion for Mary, which increases everywhere, gives us positive hope for her efficacious help and mighty protection in all our dangers."

This is the opinion of Rome regarding La Salette. Our last two great Pontiffs have lavished upon that blessed Shrine all kinds of spiritual favors, and lately, upon the occasion of the fiftieth anniversay of the Apparition, Leo XIII granted a Jubilee to the diocese of Grenoble, and to all the dioceses that asked for this favor. We have seen everwhere, throughout the hundreds of Sanctuaries of our Lady of La Salette a remarkable concourse of the faithful mingling their prayers and tears with those of the sorrowing Virgin, in order to avert the chastisements due to our sins. At one single Shrine of our Lady of

La Salette, in Belgium, thirty thousand Pilgrims were gathered together to celebrate the Golden Jubilee of the merciful Apparition.

In 1855, one year after this book was first published, another illustrious prelate, Monsignor Dupuch, first Bishop of Algiers, wrote that the devotion of La Salette is not a local but a universal one, and like a majestic tree, it must spread its branches all over the world. Thus, universality is a characteristic mark of this devotion.

The opinion of such men shows well they understood that great Event, and the Catholic world has since endorsed their prophetic testimony, when it erected everywhere Sanctuaries in commemoration of the Apparition.

In 1873, the monuments raised in honor of the Virgin of the Alps, numbered eight hundred, scattering chiefly throughout France, Spain, and Italy. Since that time, however, that number has greatly increased, and we may well say, that they are twice as numerous at present. Many of these Sanctuaries are found in Germany, Norway, England, Holland, Austria, Switzerland, United States, Canada, Brazil, Maurice, Martinique, Madagascar, Burma, West Indies, New Caledonia, even Dohemey, one of the darkest spots of the Black Continent, has its Sanctuary to our Lady of La Salette.

At all these shrines public novenas are made in preparation for the feast each year on the 19th of September. The pious custom of consecrating the entire month of September to our Lady of La Salette is rapidly spreading, particularly among Religious Communities. By an Indult of August, 1867, His Holiness Pius IX granted all the indulgences of the month of May to the Associates of the Confraternity of La Salette at Arles, who would keep the month of September in honor of our Lady Reconciler.

PUBLISHER'S EPILOGUE

To the 150th Anniversary Edition

Among the many apparitions of Our Lady, the one that has generated the most controversy is her appearance at La Salette to Peter Maximin Giraud and Frances Melanie Mathieu (Calvat), aged eleven and fourteen. It occurred back in 1846 and even now, 150 years later, the obscurity surrounding the message of La Salette remains. One of the factors which has contributed to that obscurity is that of the lives of the two witnesses after the apparition. Somehow they do not fit the mental picture we have formed of seers in general and how they should conduct themselves.

Thus, for instance, St. Catherine Labouré was already a professed nun when the Blessed Mother appeared to her in 1830. Bernadette Soubirous, the peasant girl of Lourdes, has also been canonized. Of course St. Bernadette had the benefit of an understanding parish priest who guided her gently toward the religious life. Lucia dos Santos of Fatima also entered the convent and still remains a nun. On the other hand, Francisco and Jacinta, the other two children of Fatima, died early. Thus we have no way of knowing how these two would have behaved, for example, in the wake of Vatican II.

However, as far as La Salette is concerned, Rome has spoken on the authenticity of Our Lady's apparition. Therefore we cannot impugn the secrets confided to the children by invoking the principle that the credibility of the message depends to some extent on the credibility of the messenger or messengers. On the contrary, we Catholics ought to consider the lives of the two seers as part of the evidence to be used in support of, and not against, the message of La Salette. We are helped considerably here by the current unparalleled crisis in the Church, which many believe to be a sign

MELANIE AT THE AGE OF 72

of the age of the Antichrist. Moreover, we cannot limit our scrutiny solely to the words uttered or written by the seers who, over the years, have actually seen the Blessed Virgin, while refraining from trying to gain whatever meaning their lives might hold for us. To do that is to do injustice to the many others who, though never experiencing a heavenly visitation, and thereby having no message to proclaim, were nevertheless used by God to warn future generations. One such figure was St. Benedict Joseph Labré, the vermin-ridden beggar who crisscrossed Europe in the seventeenth century. It is now held that he was a herald of divine compassion for the victims of the Age of the Enlightenment and the French Revolution. Again, his life has been interpreted as God's way of warning that same generation about the spiritual pestilence that was in store for them.

What then can we learn from the lives of the two seers of La Salette? The Mother of God prophesied that great devastation would permeate the Church and afflict her even at the highest levels. Prophecies, be it noted, become clear only when the time of their fulfillment has come. Therefore, will the lives of the two seers unfold meanings — for the generation of the Antichrist — that have eluded previous generations? In Appendix, Note C, there is given an account of their conduct after the apparition. Melanie was found dead in her room on December 15, 1904. Biographical accounts indicate that she died without receiving the last rites at the time of her death. But should that not be considered, as in the case of St. Benedict Labré, as God's way of letting us know in advance how millions would suffer a similar fate during and in the wake of the reign of the Antichrist, which, in point of fact, was the subject of the secret confided to Melanie by Our Lady? Also, do not millions of unborn infants die, not just without the benefit of the last rites, but without ever having drawn their first breath? Again, if Melanie left the convent, does it not serve as a portent of the mass exodus of the religious from convents and monasteries, such as we have witnessed since Vatican II? But of course there is this difference. The priests and nuns who have left in the thousands during the present generation have done so for reasons entirely different from those of Melanie.

As for Maximin, we excerpt the following from the same source. "...we find him (Maximin), successively a medical student, a papal Zouave, a Government official in Paris, a merchant etc...." Maximin, it is said, became a shiftless youth. While his own generation might have had difficulty with that aspect of his life, can we not accept it as a foretaste of what would happen? Since Vatican II have we experienced any permanence anywhere — in the Church *or* in our social and political institutions? The spectacle of millions of refugees today, shifting here and there all over the world, is Maximin multiplied countless times over. Maximin became a merchant, buying and selling, a career that might be construed as being unworthy of a true seer. But would not that be considered as God's way of informing that the whole world, during the reign of the Antichrist, might turn out to be a gigantic shopping mall, where the chief human concern will be buying and selling (Sundays not excepted) the earthly goods that serve as palliatives to modern man's hunger for God?

Once we have seen the symbolic significance of the lives of the seers, as no doubt foreshadowing the precarious lives of our own generation, we can better understand the content of the warnings they passed on to us. Along with the public message associated with the apparition, there is also the secret of Melanie, and it is this that has generated the most controversy. Its indictment of the moral evils of our age, and in particular of members of the Church, is so devastating that ecclesiastical authorities understandably reacted with extreme caution. In 1915 the Holy Office went so far as to issue a decree prohibiting written commentaries on the message, while at the same time reiterating the Church's approval of devotion to Our Lady of La Salette. Since Melanie's death occurred eleven years before that decree, we do not know how she would have conducted herself had she been alive when it was issued. Would she have ceased all discussion of the message that she felt called by Our Lady to make known to the world, or would she have appealed the case to Rome in order to be freer to continue her mission?

It is here that Melanie's life, ending as it did before 1915, will enlighten us. Some writers, such as Msgr. John S. Kennedy in his *Light on the Mountain*, speculated that there were certain weaknesses in Melanie herself that served to weaken the impact of her mission. Others, especially in more recent years, have focussed on the outstanding qualities of her personality and have described her as a saint. Furthermore, these latter see the difficulties that she experienced with certain ecclesiastical figures — even while she was encouraged and offered moral support by other Church authorities — as being an inevitable consequence of the awesome message that she was called by Heaven to proclaim. It is this latter conviction that seems to have been gaining momentum in recent years, and is shared by the staff of Preserving Christian Publications, Inc., thereby prompting the present reprinting of Archbishop Ullathorne's book.

It was precisely because of that awesome message that she was called to make known that Melanie suffered persecution and experienced opposition to such an extent that many were left with doubts regarding her character. But what about the decree of 1915? Had Rome finally decided to side with her accusers, in spite of the favorable response that she had received from Pope Pius IX, Leo XIII and St. Pius X? Here we are dealing with the ultimate mystery of La Salette and its seer. If Our Lady divided her message into parts, one being public and the other being secret, she must have done so for a very specific reason. Precisely because it was a secret, the latter part of the message was not intended to be known and understood immediately, but only, in the final analysis,. at the time when the prophecies that it contained were reaching their final fulfillment. That fulfillment had not yet taken place in 1915, and therefore it could be said that the Church acted wisely by postponing public discussion of the Secret of La Salette. At this time of the 150th anniversary of the apparition, however, Catholics throughout the world have once again been circulating and discussing the text of Melanie's secret. In so doing are these members of the Church acting in defiance of ecclesiastical authority? That is, is the decree of 1915 still fully in force, so that public discussion of the Secret's contents would constitute an act of disobedience and defiance?

Such questions as these can only be answered by the Church herself, and therefore we must leave it to the Church's highest authority to answer them. In anticipation of her action, however, we call our readers' attention to an important principle in law, in this case the law of the Church, which concerns the abrogation or modification of laws in the light of circumstances developing subsequent to their promulgation. It is the principle of contrary custom. When, with the passage of time, certain laws cease widely to be observed in all their rigor, not because the subjects are disobedient and defiant, but because changing circumstances no longer make them binding in the way they were at the time of enactment, that contrary custom is seen by legal experts as the equivalent of the abrogation of the law.

We as publishers have no authority to declare a law or decree abrogated by custom. But what we, as members of the Holy Catholic Church, do sense, however, is the following: a growing number of Catholics are becoming increasingly convinced that specific prophecies contained in Melanie's secret have now been fulfilled, in the course of the lives of the present generation of Catholics.

These circumstances did not exist at the time of Rome's decree in 1915, but these Catholics contend that they do exist at the present time. Had the faithful been allowed to discuss the secret's contents freely in 1915, immense confusion might have resulted within the Church, precisely because specific prophecies it contained were not yet fulfilled, and therefore there were insufficient facts available to interpret them correctly. But today the circumstances have changed considerably, and therefore the reasons prompting the law are to be viewed in the light of those present circumstances, that is, of today's unparalleled crisis in the history of the Church.

When, in 1946, the La Salette Fathers celebrated the centenary of the apparition, they did so with the blessing and encouragement of the reigning pope, His Holiness Pope Pius XII. This year, marking the 150th anniversary, will certainly not pass without the Catholic world paying attention once again to the significance of Our Lady's message, made to Melanie and Maximin. It is our desire to contribute in some way to that observance, and we do so with this reprinting of Archbishop Ullathorne's book. In undertaking such action we leave it to the Church herself to make the ultimate judgment, regarding the secret messages that the Mother of God transmitted to the two seers at La Salette.